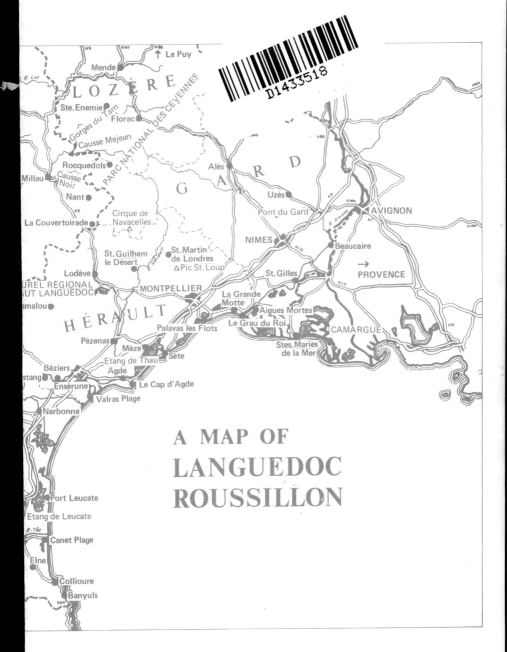

A MAP OF
LANGUEDOC
ROUSSILLON

History, People and Places in

LANGUEDOC
ROUSSILLON

Maison Carrée, Nîmes

History,
People and Places
in
LANGUEDOC
ROUSSILLON

Neil Lands

SPURBOOKS LIMITED

Published By
Spurbooks Ltd
6 Parade Court
Bourne End
Buckinghamshire

ISBN   0 904978 00 1

Typesetting by Inforum Ltd, Portsmouth
Printed and bound in Great Britain by
Redwood Burn Limited
Trowbridge and Esher

FOR ALEXANDRA AND CLAIRE

Contents

Acknowledgements

The Author and Publishers would like to thank the following people for their help in the preparation of this book.

Pauline Hallam and Jenifer Cornet of the French Government Tourist Office in London; Mme and Mlle. Chantal Larinier of Valras-Plage; Yves Hoffman and Pierre Belaman of Perpignan; M.P. Streat and Terry Adolph of Blue Line Cruisers (France), Castelnaudary; M.A.P. Robert of Castelnau le Nez; The London Library; Terry Brown for help with the maps; and Estelle Huxley for assistance in manuscript preparation.

Illustrations

1

An Historial Introduction

Once upon a time, a troubadour sat astride his horse on a bridge over the River Loire, and looked across at the North bank. There lay fame, in the Court at Paris, or in the castles of the great Dukes, in whose service lay riches and renown. Behind lay Languedoc, a land which, as a French King could ruefully remark, offered only wine and gaiety. The troubadour, without regret, turned his back on fame and fortune, and rode South into the sunshine, on a journey so gay that, so they say, even his horse sang.

I'd like to have heard that!

If you will take a little time now to study the end-paper maps, you will see that the modern Languedoc-Roussillon lies between the Eastern Pyrénées and the course of the Rhône. In the troubadour's time, during the twelfth and thirteenth centuries, Languedoc was a much larger area, covering most of the land south of the Loire. It is one of the few areas that has taken its name from the tongue spoken there, rather than the other way round. South of the Loire, they spoke the *langue d'Oc*, where the French *ouil*, later *oui*, for 'yes', was rendered by *oc*. To this day, the people are known as the Occitans, the people of the Languedoc, although more popularly, as the region forms part of the Midi, the people are generally referred to as the *Meridional*.

Traditionally the *Meridional* are a happy-go-lucky, cheerful people, much given to wine, song, and insurrection. They inhabit a landscape of great beauty and variety, blessed with magnificent weather, and of growing economic importance. It was not always so. The history of Languedoc-Roussillon, until quite recent times, has been bloody.

One must appreciate, for any comprehension of French history, that for many centuries after the accession of the first French King, Hugh Capet, the King of France only ruled directly in the Ile de France, an area around Paris. He was, indeed, sometimes called the King of Paris.

13

Through the Cévennes

The history of the French kings is, therefore, a long story of attempts to extend their power over their nobles. Geographically, the France of history was not the France of today. France expanded to her present frontiers, gradually, over the centuries, and in that time the people in the provinces of what is now Metropolitan France, had time to develop cultures and customs of their own. They are still French. They are also themselves. Of nowhere is this more true than Languedoc-Roussillon. Dramatic events marked the history of the region since the thirteenth century, and left scars that can be detected today.

The first, in the early thirteenth century, was the Albigensian Crusade, of which the most significant political result was the absorption of the Languedoc into the French King's domain. Until then it had been the fiefdom of the Counts of Toulouse, who in riches and military power, out-matched their overlord in Paris. They were a tolerant and well-loved house, and gave their protection to an heretical sect called the Cathars, which was very strong in the South, and based in the town of Albi.

This sect was anathema to the Catholic Church, which, in view of its doctrine, is hardly surprising. Briefly, the sect held that man was physically vile and a creation of the devil, for God could never have created a creature capable of such evil. They maintained, moreover, that all men, and even the fallen angels, could obtain redemption by leading a pure life. The true Cathar, (the word is derived from the Greek, meaning pure or clean) was a vegetarian, refrained from sexual intercourse even in marriage, and devoted his life to prayer and the conversion of others to his beliefs. Those who by abstinence and prayer became the *Perfecti,* were assured of a place in Heaven, not by God's mercy, but by right. This was a grave heresy, and after the Papal missionaries had failed to combat it effectively, a crusade was launched against them, which after a brutal period of forty years, wiped out the Cathars and the House of Toulouse, to absorb Languedoc into the Kingdom of France in 1229. The Cathars were finally extinguished in 1244.

*   *   *

The other part of the region, Roussillon, was a possession of Spain until 1659. The Pyrénées, during the Middle Ages, divided nothing. Roussillon and the Cerdagne were important fiefs of the great prince, the Count of Barcelona. The people of the Roussillon are therefore Catalan, the French of Catalonia, and between 1276 and 1344, the Roussillon formed part of the short-lived Kingdom of Majorca.

Roussillon was almost the last great area to fall to the French crown, pushing their frontier back to the natural defensive boundary of the Pyrénées.

The Kings of Spain had other lands or possessions in the South, notably the town of Montpellier, and with various ups and downs, continued to hold these until, in 1642, Cardinal Richelieu layed siege to Perpignan, and when it fell, absorbed Roussillon into the French crown. But this, you will note, was not until the middle of the seventeenth century, and the Frenchmen of the Roussillon remain proud of their Catalan history and customs to this very day.

Between these two events came the Wars of Religion, which tore at France in the sixteenth century. Languedoc has a tradition of resistance to central authority. It supported the Cathars, and when the reformed religion spread into France, they took to it almost to a man. Indeed, the Protestant Church is well represented in Languedoc-Roussillon to this day. Richelieu struck the first blow against the Huguenots of the South when he deprived them of many of the privileges enjoyed under Henri IV's Edict of Nantes. He took away their places of security, destroyed the castles of their leaders, and left them only the right to practise their religion, and this they soon lost, in the reign of Louis XIV.

When Louis XIV revoked the Edict of Nantes in 1689, most Huguenots fled abroad. Not so those of the Languedoc. Some fled indeed, but others took to the hills of the Cévennes and, in what became the Camisard revolt, held out against the Crown for over seventy years. Already you see the vision of a truculent, free people, resisting oppression down the centuries.

Of course, the history of the region goes back beyond the existence of the French Kings. This was Southern Gaul that saw the Greek and Phoenician seamen, and traded with them out of ports like Agde. Then the Romans came and established themselves at Narbonne, at Béziers, and most of all, at Nîmes, which contains some of the finest Roman remains in all Europe, and still cherishes that antique, classical connection.

Rome fell in the fifth century, but here it was the Vandals, and later the Visigoths who over-ran their possessions, not the Teutonic

16

The 'joust' at Adge; Hérault

Franks, who came over the Rhine to possess, and eventually give their name to, the land of the French. The Franks then came down, across the Loire, and drove the Visigoths into Spain. All these invasions have left marks on the sunny face of the Languedoc, and if much has changed, the people and the sun remain.

Today, Languedoc-Roussillon is made up of the *départements* of Lozère, Gard, Hérault and Aude, which comprise all that is left of Languedoc, and Pyrénées Orientales which almost exactly coincides with the former Catalan Roussillon. On the one side lies Provence, and on the other, Spain. To the North lies the Massif Central, and the land runs South to the Mediterranean Sea.

After the Revolution, as part of the process of breaking with the past, the Revolutionary Government abolished the old provinces and replaced them with a number of *départements*, usually naming them after the principal local river. As French rivers have remarkably pretty names, this was an excellent idea, but one which has never quite caught on. The French people are no less traditionally-minded than the British, and they remained stubbornly Norman, or

Poitivan, or Occitan, or Catalan. The new regions, based on the old Provincial names, were officially created anew in 1960, mainly to make larger economic units and attract development capital and tourism; also, one likes to think, to mark the submission of Government to the ingrained loyalties of the provincial people.

*   *   *

What is it like, this Languedoc-Roussillon? When Wordsworth wrote:

> *Two voices there are,*
> *One of the sea and one of the mountains,*
> *And each a mighty voice...*

he might have been thinking of the Midi.

It is warm, windy, bleached by the hot summer sun, lashed by torrents, and jagged with the mountains that back the coastal plain; those peaks with entrancing names, the Corbières, the Minervois, the Montagne Noir, the Pyrénées, and the marvellous Cévennes. It is a land of viniculture with mile upon mile of vineyards covering the land. It contains the desolate Causses, and the spectacular Gorges of the Tarn. There are natural wonders like the brilliant grottos of Clamouse and Demoiselles, or the beautiful Cirque de Navacelles. The climate is Mediterranean, very hot in summer, mild in spring and autumn, but in such a large country with such a variety of geography, there is considerable local variation in the weather. In winter, snow lies on the Pyrénées until April, and it can be bitter on the wild, open Causses. The rivers, shallow and sparkling in summer, become dangerous torrents in winter.

The land is quite beautiful. It has the sun, of course, which can gild even a dreary Northern city, but here the land glows. It is a land of red roofs, green vines, rose-coloured castles, blue sea and clear sky. It has history, and it has romance. It even has innovation.

Until the late 1950s, the coastal area was avoided by travellers because, however much the attraction, there was one formidable snag — the mosquito. I do not know if they have ever eaten a man alive, but they can certainly have a very good try. In the shallow brackish *étangs* or lakes, which lie behind the coastline, mosquitos bred and swarmed. Clearly, if the area was to be developed, they had

18

14th-century packhorse bridge in the Cirque de Navacelles

The pyramids of La Grande Motte

to go. It took over ten years, but the mosquito was finally vanquished and where they once swarmed, in their place today swarm tourists, yachtsmen, residents and summer visitors. The whole coastline is one long beach, with perfect bathing in the warm blue sea.

The coast, from the Rhône to the Pyrénées, is being developed by a chain of new towns, some with spectacular architecture, and none quite like any of the others. La Grande-Motte, Cap d'Agde, Port Leucate, Gruissan and Port Barcarès, are a paradise for yachtsmen, and sun-lovers, and from all over Europe the pale folk of the Northern cities are coming to buy homes and moor their craft. Even the old ports like lovely Sète, bustling Valras, or quaint Collioure, are putting out the flags for an ever growing number of visitors.

But it's a big place. There is lots of room, and the most popular beach is never crowded. Behind the beaches lie the great blue-green hills, with quite different attractions for sport and leisure, from fishing to pot-holing, walking, hunting, riding, canoeing, or more to my taste, just enjoying the solitude that this vast area has to offer in abundance. The attraction of Languedoc-Roussillon is in the great variety it offers. A variety of scenery, from flat sandy coast to high green

20

mountain, a variety of large town and miniscule village, of history and architecture. It can also claim to possess some of the great engineering achievements of former times, such as the great aquaduct of the Pont du Gard, or later, Paul Riquet's Canal du Midi. The traveller to Languedoc-Roussillon cannot be bored.

*   *   *

The people who live in Languedoc-Roussillon earn their living principally from wine. The area is the largest wine producer in France, and the quality is steadily improving. The range of wine available is remarkable, for it seems that every village produces its own local brew, and for the visitor the local wine is usually the best. Apart from wine, the area relies increasingly on tourism and is developing fast as a holiday region.

For the British visitor, the region lies some six hundred miles from the Channel ports, just off the main route to Spain. You need a car to tour Languedoc, and the shortest route down by the recently completed auto-route is a two-day drive. You can ship the car by train from Boulogne or Paris to Narbonne or Avignon, which, all-in, is not too expensive, and at least you arrive in the area fresh. More settled travellers can fly to Perpignan or Montpellier, and both cities are good centres for touring the surrounding country.

Languedoc-Roussillon, thank goodness, isn't chic. It has fashionable resorts, of course, like Cap d'Agde and La Grande-Motte, while Montpellier, Nîmes and Béziers are towns as pleasant and as full of good shops as one could find anywhere in France. Mercifully though, there is little of that studied sophistication that you encounter on the Côte d'Azur, or the sugary prettiness of Provence. Languedoc-Roussillon is a region close to the land, the sea and the mountains, and it has solid appeal, rather than a facile charm.

One can only hope that some of those thousands stampeding over the frontier into Spain, will pause and visit Languedoc-Roussillon. It has much to offer, and they won't be disappointed.

*   *   *

This book is about the modern region, as defined by *départements*, and will stay fairly strictly within those boundaries. Old Languedoc, as already mentioned, was much bigger and had its capital in Toulouse. Nowadays, Montpellier has that honour, and we shall go there, but only fleetingly, for, to be honest, I don't like big cities. With the best intentions they are slaves to the motor-car, and whatever charm they formerly possessed is now being rapidly and irrevocably eroded.

Here we are concerned with three facets of the region; the history, the people and the places. All are interlinked, and need not be separated too distinctly. The history has been touched on lightly as a basic introduction in order to make future references clear. The people are as they are, and one must take them as one finds them. I confess to being amused by travellers who eulogise about people of other lands. Those mystical people who are always gay, laughing, dancing, drinking, loving, or waving their arms about. What blanket comment! People in general may have national or regional characteristics, but individually they are human beings, with all the problems and interests of human beings everywhere. It is not necessary to put them under any kind of microscope where they can be closely observed as a slightly less serious form of life!

If I had to generalise about the *Méridional*, I would say that they seem very good humoured and of rather small stature. Few great historical figures have made their mark in Languedoc-Roussillon, and yet the land is not without heroes; St. Louis, the Cathars, Molière, sundry Kings, Dukes, Templar Knights and Princes, Colbert and Riquet, Vauban and Viollet-le-Duc, Richelieu and Cinq-Mars. There is no lack of characters to fill this stage.

We will be looking in some detail at the history of the region, as we travel about. It is long and fascinating, but above all it is intricate. Travellers and amateur historians tend to think of history on the ground as a vertical development. First, so the thinking goes, came the Greeks, and they built the foundations, then the Romans built on that, then came the Visigoths, and so on. This is convenient historical shorthand, but unfortunately, for the Languedoc-Roussillon, it just won't do.

The only point that needs to be stressed now, and remembered throughout, is that for much of history the Pyrénées which now divide—or rather join—France and Spain, divided nothing. For the history of the region ignores present day frontiers and flows across the region, to and fro, in an embattled and bloody tide.

Places? Well, there are lots of places. Old ones like Carcassonne

Romanesque Cloister, St Michel de Cuxa, Roussillon

and Aigues-Mortes, new ones like La Grande Motte and Cap d'Agde. Big like Montpellier or small, like St. Guilhem-le-Désert, with its beautiful church. Languedoc-Roussillon is a treasure house of Romanesque church architecture, which has nothing to do with the Romans, dating from between the tenth and twelfth centuries. It is a romantic style, rich in carving, allegorical designs, and mythical figures.

Places are really pegs on which to hang the trip. The real pleasure of travelling is simply travelling, and while, in the following pages a genuine effort is made to describe many of the best places to visit in Languedoc-Roussillon, I hope it is not a comprehensive list, and that people can find their own special places, those mystical discoveries "where the (other) tourists don't go".

The best way to find such places is just to wander about. We must assume a car and a few weeks holiday. The rest is up to the visitor. Let him go where he will and find his own version of the country, for

23

travelling is probably the last freedom left. The game is still to wander, preferably abroad, preferably alone. The limits are time, money, and experience, none of which, within limits, is insuperable, and the rewards are, well, rewarding. The theory that travel broadens the mind is more correct than the fact that it flattens the feet. Who has not crawled wearily around some endless museum? Yet, without the spur of departure, or the surprise of discovery, who would trouble to learn and enjoy all that is to be known about the world around us? Even on this trip, we can learn about architecture, ponder the fate of the Knights Templar, learn to play *boule,* or dance the *Sardane,* hear many old stories, and probe one still sensitive mystery, to name but a few. All this is, perhaps, just possible at home, but then where is the sun, the heat, the local flavour, the wonderful world of abroad?

In a piece by Hilaire Belloc there is an engaging character called Peter Wanderwide, who claimed that extensive travel in this world was an excellent qualification for touring Heaven in the next.

Almighty God will surely cry
St. Michael, who is this that stands
With Ireland in his dubious eye
And Périgord between his hands?

And on his arm the stirrup thongs
And in his gait the narrow seas
And in his mouth Burgundian songs
But in his heart the Pyrenees.

Isn't that nice? Doesn't that ring! It expresses exactly, the indefinable pleasures of travel, of simply getting about.

Before we go, a word about this book. It takes restraint to keep a written story of a trip from being an account of a tour round the local churches. Be they never so beautiful or historic—and Languedoc is a shrine of the Romanesque style—there is more to life than can be found in the cloister. Even the old monks suspected that! Certainly one must visit some of the churches, and we shall sort out the best, but if the area has variety, then so must the book.

This will, I hope, be a light-hearted account of a trip through a region of great appeal. Some of the stories are anything but funny, but on the other hand, this was the land of the troubadours, and it is difficult to plod around continually in a state of earnest gloom, how-

La Couvertoirade of the Knights Templar

Porte Narbonnaise Carcassonne

ever traditional. The woolly-sock school of traveller is on the way out, and enjoyment is no longer a voyager's version of *lèse-majesté*.

It was, I believe, Oscar Wilde, who, when in New York was taken by his hosts to visit the city's only genuine English-American style pub. He gazed around at the brasses, the old posters, the chintz, and the warm beer, and groaned. "Oh God!" he said, "How I hate feeling at home, when I'm abroad." So do I.

2

From the Rhône to the Cévennes

The Rhône divides Languedoc from Provence, and as it lies on the eastern bank, Avignon is really outside the area covered by this book. However, it would be a foolish and incredibly restrained traveller who could arrive at Avignon in the early hours and depart without at least a look at the town's two historic landmarks, the Palace of the Popes and the famous Pont d'Avignon.

Besides, to strike a more prosaic note, the restaurant at the Rail Terminal is always very crowded when the over-night motor-rail train arrives, and a much quicker coffee and croissant can be obtained at any of the cafés in the centre of the town. Avignon shopkeepers rise at dawn, working no doubt on the theory that the early bird catches the tourist. It is a kind and useful practice all the same, and puts you in the right mood to see the sights.

We have to remember, throughout this book, that France is a recent construction. Avignon did not become part of France until the time of the French Revolution, before which it belonged to the Papacy. In previous centuries the Kings of France hovered on the far bank of the Rhône, regarding Avignon with a lustful eye and, French Kings being French Kings, from time to time the temptation proved too much and they surged across the river and took it for themselves. However, as it belonged to the Pope, in the end the Most Christian King usually gave it back. The Popes not only owned Avignon, but from 1305 until 1377 actually lived there.

Seven Popes lived and ruled in Avignon during the period which the Roman Church refers to as the "Babylonian Captivity". These Popes were, of course, French, and largely the creatures of the French King, and although one of them, Urban V, became a Saint, the first, Clement V, was the tool of Philip the Fair, aiding him in the persecution of the Knights Templar, which will be discussed later. Provence, in which Avignon lies, was ceded to the French Crown in 1481.

This was all a long time ago, and the years of Papal occupancy have left behind a most magnificent medieval palace, and a fine circular defensive wall around the old town. The Papal residence does not look much like a palace. It resembles, far more, a grim medieval fortress, and this it is, and with reason. The Popes lived in Avignon for much of the Hundred Years War, that long and bitter dispute between the two great sons of the Church, which the Popes struggled mightily to keep out of and, on at least one occasion, a huge and greedy army of professional soldiers, the Free Companies, camped around the walls, and had to be paid to go away. They had come, they said, to see the Pope and have some of his money.

This was in 1360, after the Treaty of Bretigny engineered a brief pause in the hostilities of the Hundred Years War. After a while, the English mercenaries went off with John Hawkwood to fight in Spain, and the Pope breathed again. The Papal treasure, though, was not the only attraction. In the Middle Ages, Avignon was an arms centre for the manufacture of, and trade in, suits of mail and various types of weapons, and the town is still an industrial centre.

The town itself is interesting, surrounded by a medieval wall, built about 1320, standing about twenty feet high with a total length of three miles. From one point juts the famous Pont. The pressure of population has reduced the thickness of the wall considerably and it is now very thin, the former buttresses giving place to a narrow interior ring-road, while many breaches have been made through it to give access to traffic.

However, it is still attractive, and inside, the deep shade offered by the tall plane trees along the streets, makes a welcome change on a warm morning. The centre square, or Place de L'Horloge, is just by the Palace of the Popes. In the square, notice the statue to Crillon, the best fighting general of Henry of Navarre. He was born in Avignon, and although a Catholic, was a King's man, and served Henry loyally against the Catholic League.

The Palace itself is huge, covering an area of thirty acres. It had to be large; a whole Court lived in it permanently for the best part of a hundred years. It is set back on the far side of the square, and the full proportions are thus on view. It is mainly of fourteenth-century construction, being built between 1334 and 1352 with many later additions. It is a fine place, well worth a visit.

The Cathedral of Notre Dame contains the tomb of Pope John XXII, and a great number of chapels, vestibules and throne rooms, all lavishly decorated with tapestries. Nearby are various museums, the Musée Calvet being particularly worth a visit, having a huge library, and opening early. It also has a fine picture gallery including local masters of the eighteenth century. The Popes moved to Avignon, exhausted by the continual riots in Rome. The fact that their stay resulted in this magnificent Palace gives us something to thank the turbulent Romans for.

Not far from the Palace lies the Rhône, and reaching across the waters, the famous Pont.

* * *

All French children, and many English ones, know the song which says:

> *Sur le Pont d'Avignon*
> *L'on y dansait tous en ronde.*

It comes as a shock, therefore, to find that the bridge has only half its span, and ends abruptly in the middle of the river. What sort of dance can have caused that to happen? In fact the bridge was a pack-horse bridge, and any dancing took place on the island, by the bridge, in the middle of the river. The bridge was built in the late twelfth century by St. Bénézet, who founded an Order of Monks devoted to bridge building. It collapsed three centuries later, but in that short time it gave France an enduring and catchy little folk song. It seems a pity that the bridge cannot be rebuilt, to forge another link between Provence and Languedoc. Meanwhile, Avignon is the centre, each year, for a celebrated Arts Festival, and is in this case an excellent starting point for a tour of the Languedoc.

To start the sweep north at the most southern point, you take the road out of Avignon to Tarascon. This is a pretty run, through green countryside, with the rocky escarpment of La Montagnette rising up on the right.

At Tarascon, by the bridge, one can pause in the shade of the castle walls, and look across the wide Rhône to Beaucaire on the Languedoc bank. Beaucaire lies under cover, with only the roofs visible, feeling well protected by the presence of the huge and lofty castle which stands above the town. The castle of Beaucaire is a shell, gutted by the orders of Cardinal Richelieu, but for centuries it defied the other,

Beaucaire

still well-preserved, castle of Tarascon. Tarascon is remembered in French literature, by Daudet's amiable idiot, *Tartarin de Tarascon*. Tarascon was also the home of the Count of Provence, known in French history as Good King René. He was called King, for, being of the House of Anjou, he had a claim to the throne of Naples, and he was called 'good' because he had no interest in war or plunder or the other pastimes of the medieval lord, but preferred to listen to the poetry and music of the famous Provençal *jongleurs.*

On his death in 1480 he ceded Provence to the French King, and another barrier to French expansion was swept away. The Rhône had divided France from the Holy Roman Empire for so long that, so it is said, bargemen on the river would indicate their destination with shouts of "*Royame*" (Kingdom) for France, and "*Empire*" for the ports on the eastern bank. There was no bridge between Tarascon and Beaucaire in those days. Today a fine modern bridge sweeps you over the wide flood in no time, and you arrive at last in Languedoc.

*   *   *

Beaucaire is a nice little town, with narrow medieval streets, full of commercial bustle around the covered market. In the Middle Ages, the Fair at Beaucaire was famous and the town still has extensive trading connections. It is the head port for the Rhône-Sète canal, constructed in the seventeenth century, and has a fine *Mairie,* or town hall, built in the reign of Louis XIV, which carries the rayed emblem of the Sun King on the upper walls. Beaucaire is dominated by the castle, which was built by Raymond VI of Toulouse in the thirteenth century, extended over the following centuries and destroyed by Richelieu. The parts that remain, the tower and curtain walls, are of the fifteenth and early sixteenth centuries. Richelieu had, as one of the planks in his overall policy, a determination to destroy the power of the provincial French nobility. They were directed to dismantle their castles unless these were on the frontiers. Those who disobeyed the edict had their castles razed by the Cardinal troops, and one such was Beaucaire. From Beaucaire it is a short and pleasant run through fruit fields, north, towards Uzès, and the Pont du Gard.

The Romans have left many memorials in Southern France, not least in the very name of Provence, which comes from their "*Provincia Romana*", but none is as magnificent and enduring as the Pont du Gard. It was, and remains, a wonder of the ancient world. It isn't really a bridge. It was built as an aquaduct to carry water to Nîmes, from Uzès, a distance of over thirty miles. The aquaduct has disappeared and the bridge portion over the River Gard is all that is left. It was built about the year 20 B.C. on the orders of Agrippa, when

The Pont du Gard

Nîmes was expanding as a settlement after the Octavian Wars. It is nearly two hundred feet high and of three tiers, the top one carrying the water channel.

It is a pity that so much of the original aquaduct has been taken away, but the medieval builder can hardly be blamed if he used ancient foundations, long since disused, as quarries for his necessary supply of dressed stone. The labour involved in the cutting of fresh stone from the rock must have been immense, and the temptation to raid an existing supply too much to resist. Many monasteries in Britain suffered in similar ways after the Reformation — indeed much of their value lay in their material — but it is a pity, for the old buildings had style, and too few examples remain of really classical and, as in the case of the Pont du Gard, functional architecture.

From the Pont du Gard we go north again towards Uzès, through farming country. The open fields are fenced with tall hedges or pine or yew to make windbreaks. This is *mistral* country, and when it

The Pont du Gard (another view)

blows only these hedges prevent the wind scouring the earth off the very rocks below.

The *mistral* is a wearisome wind that funnels down the Rhône Valley, hard on the land and the tempers of the people. Legend has it that the *mistral* is so trying on the temper that crimes committed while it blew, even murder, were viewed much more sympathetically by the magistrates than at other times. There is no such recorded licence for crimes committed under the influence of the other great local wind, the Pyrenean *tramontane*, so I imagine that the *mistral* indulgence is a piece of wishful thinking.

The *mistral* has, however, influenced the local architecture. Notice the low profile of the houses, hunched round to the south, with all the blank rear walls turned into the face of the wind. The country grows fruit, cherries, peaches, grapes, oranges, all clustering to ripen in the sun, and can be purchased in the local shops. The quality is excellent, and my way at least, is always paved with cherry stones.

Uzès is a striking town in the valley of the Alzon. The town suffered in the Wars of Religion, and was largely rebuilt in the seventeenth century, although some medieval relics remain, notably the market. The castle has a remarkable hunting room where the walls are furred with antlers, trophies of a Lady of Uzès some seventy years ago, who must have decimated the local wildlife to obtain such a collection.

The castle, or Duché, as it is called, lies in the centre of the town and was the seat of the Duc d'Uzès, the premier Duke of France. It is better to park here and walk to the other sights, the Cathedral and the twelfth century Tour Fenestrelle, before heading north again to Alès.

On the way, just past the little village of Baron, the road leaps up to a crest, and you can see, far away and blue, the mountains of the Cévennes on the horizon. They appear constantly thereafter, until you arrive at Alès, the capital of the Cévennes; or so Alès describes itself. It is a busy town, quite large, of about fifty thousand people, and is very much a tourist centre. It has a number of good hotels, notably the Luxembourg and the Grand, the latter overlooking the River Gardon. It was here that I noticed that the *département* of Gard seemed to have a very long and wandering river on its hands, and took myself off to the Tourist Office for an explanation. It appears that there are no less than *seven* rivers all called Gard, or Gardon, within the *département,* which makes it simple for the cartographers, but causes a problem for the traveller. The reader must appreciate, therefore, that from now on, when I refer to the Gard or Gardon, it means *a* river, rather than *the* river.

At Alès in 1629, Richelieu, on behalf of Louis XIII issued the Edict of Grace. This deprived the Huguenots of many of the privileges they had received from Henri IV, under the Edict of Nantes. They lost their right to have fortified places, and were open to conversion from Catholic missionaries. They were, however, left their free-

Anduze, gateway to the Cévennes

dom of worship, and it took the Revocation of the Edict of Nantes by Louis XIV to drive the Huguenots either abroad or into rebellion.

Alès is an old town, and the older part of the town, away from the modernised river bank, was built by Vauban in the late seventeenth century. Alès stands on the banks of a River Gardon and industriously promotes tourism in the Cévennes and in Ardèche. Neither is far away; the River Ardèche, which is a great centre for canoeing and water sports is only some twenty-five miles from Alès. Passing through Alès and turning back on one's tracks a little, will bring you quickly to Anduze. Anduze, although much smaller, has the edge over Alès when it comes to the setting, for this little town is situated in a bowl of the Cévennes, in an open valley, a little gem, surrounded by cliffs; the perfect gateway to the mountains beyond.

The Cévennes is a range of mountains, running roughly from south-west to north-east across Languedoc, for about eighty miles, between the great Causses or plateau and the gorse-covered *garrigue* from La Couvertoirade up to near Mount Lozère. The mountains are not particularly high, topping out at about three thousand feet

36

with Mount Lozère the highest at five and a half thousand feet. The range is not particularly wide, being about forty miles across at the widest part. Where they score is in having great natural beauty, almost totally unspoiled, with a remarkably mild climate for most of the year, although there is much local variation and the winters can be bitter. Much of the Cévennes has been declared a National Park, thus protecting the area forever from industrialization and commercialism — we hope!

For a mountain range, the Cévennes is remarkably green and well watered, thanks to the ubiquitous Garden. These tinkling rivers, running clear over sand and gravel, are delightful in the heat of the summer day.

The Cévennes is the sort of area where, after a day spent travelling through the mountains, the visitor asks himself how he could have travelled so much before and missed it. Peter Wanderwide slipped up here, but Robert Louis Stevenson should have put the Cévennes on the map for he took a walking holiday here at the end of the last century, accompanied by a donkey. The combination should have been irresistible! In spite of his subsequent book, the Cévennes remain little known, and it would appear that the locals prefer it that way. Signs on the walls declaring *"Non aux tourists"*, and even more forceful phrases, make any wise travel writer maintain a low profile!

To see the Cévennes in every detail could take a lifetime, but a very good sample can be enjoyed by following the road over the hills from St Jean du Gard to Florac. This road, the *Corniche des Cévennes* is itself interesting, being built on the orders of Louis XIV to allow his troops into the hills and suppress the Camisard revolt.

From Anduze the road leads up to St Jean, running beside a Gard all the way. You can make an interesting side trip to the Protestant site at the Mas-Soubeyran. The Mas-Soubeyran is a museum to the Huguenots, recording the struggle of the Protestants after the Revocation of the Edict of Nantes in 1685. The effect of the Revocation was to deny the Protestants their freedom of worship and the right to practise their religion, and many promptly left France for ever. Over one hundred thousand people fled across the seas, many to England. The *Cévenoles* are a truculent lot however, and aimed to resist the Royal Edict, having no intention of quitting their native soil.

The great method used to coerce people to submit and accept Catholicism, was to billet soldiers on them, particularly dragoons, who had to be fed, horse and man, at the expense of the householder.

This was called, popularly, a *dragonnade*, and the word has remained in English and French to this day when we talk of people being 'dragooned' into some action. The Cévenoles resisted the campaign against their faith until in 1702 a particularly persistent Catholic preacher was killed. Following this, and the resulting actions of the authorities, the local Protestants rose in revolt, the so-called Camisard Rebellion, an all out civil war for two years, continuing intermittently until 1789, when liberty of worship was re-established. All over France Catholic masses are advertised outside the towns and villages. Here in the Cévennes, Protestant Church services receive similar promotion, a prosaic reminder of a stout resistance.

One of the leaders of the Revolt, Roland, had his headquarters at Mas-Soubeyran, until he was killed in 1704, and the building has been converted into a museum recording the Protestant struggle and the measures used against them. It also shows a typical Cévenole farmhouse of the period and is, all in all, a most interesting museum. The word *Mas*, which can be seen everywhere in Languedoc, really means a farm, but now is in general use to signify a country house, usually isolated, and usually small.

Bathing in the Gardon

In the summer the River Gardon is warm and shallow, with pools just deep enough for a swim, and in the mid-day heat of summer, these pools make refreshing places for picnics. The countryside hereabouts is very beautiful, the hills clothed in a thick green mantle of trees, and fruit growing in the water meadows by the river. St Jean is noted for fruit and is set on the bank of the river among orchards. A good hotel in St Jean is the Moderne, which has an excellent restaurant offering local specialities such as wild boar. At any moment one expects those Gaulish heroes, Asterix and Obelix, to walk in.

The Gard is spanned by two bridges, one of which dates from the Middle Ages. This was partly washed away about fifteen years ago, and has only just been painstakingly reconstructed. From St Jean, you follow the signs for the *Corniche des Cévennes*. This route climbs up high above the surrounding valleys of the various Gardons, and gives magnificent views over the Cévennes and the mountains of Lozère. The traveller should stop to admire the scenery as the roads are too narrow to permit much distraction from the view ahead, while driving. One quickly begins to notice fine and curious shapes among the rocks, which have been carved and moulded into strange sculptures by the action of wind and rain. By Pompidou, I was able to take out field-glasses and spend fifteen minutes in the sun, watching two eagles soaring lazily on the thermals around the mountain side. The views from the mountains around Pompidou are wonderful. Wild flowers carpet the rocky plateau and everywhere stretch the green hills. Beyond Pompidou one can see over on the left, the heights of Mont Aigoual, at over five thousand feet, the second highest mountain in the Cévennes.

The Corniche route is quite high, reaching three thousand feet in places. Up on the top, at L'Hopitalet, is a *chaos*, a curious rock formation. These chaos are by no means uncommon in Languedoc, and this is only a small one, but it was the first I had seen, and worth a stop. The rocks have been hollowed out by the elements, and fashioned into interesting sculptures. Indeed, standing on the short open grass, out in the bright sun, they looked like a very *avant-garde* sculpture exhibition.

From L'Hopitalet, the road falls steadily down to Florac, in the Valley of the Tarnon.

Florac is a pretty town, and clearly has always been so, for the name comes from the Latin *Flor-aqua*, or Water-flower. It lies at the foot of the steep cliffs of the Causse Méjean, and is backed by the

Slate-shuttered house in Florac

Boule

Cévennes. Florac is a centre for touring the regions of the Causses and the Cévennes and is near the entrance to the Gorges du Tarn. The town has two excellent hotels; the Hotel du Parc, and the Hotel Gorges du Tarn. Both offer good accommodation at reasonable prices, and the Parc is set in pleasant grounds with the restaurant on the verandah overlooking the gardens. Here, among other dishes, they serve a pleasant cheese — the *Bleu de Causse* — new to me, which is sharp, not unlike Roquefort, but considerably cheaper.

Florac was, and is, a centre for the Protestant religion in the Cévennes, and as such, suffered considerably in the Religious Wars. The local Catholic Bishop of Mende was particularly hard on Florac in the eighteenth century, and it was virtually a ghost town at the time of the Revolution. Today, with tourism and some light industry, the little town lives again, most pleasantly. Certainly the inhabitants are a friendly and hospitable lot, quick to offer the visitor a friendly word, or a game of *boule*.

Boule, or to give it its correct name, *Pétanque*, is the great preoccupation of the Midi. The traveller will see *boule* played all over

41

the Midi, on proper pitches or, more commonly, on any piece of ground.

It is a simple game, and history speculates that it was *pétanque* and not bowls that Francis Drake was playing while he awaited news of the Armada, using cannon balls for bowls. The *boules* certainly resemble them in weight and size. The idea of the game, which can be played by two players, each with three *boules*, or in two teams of three each with two *boules*, is as follows:

The first player draws a circle round his feet and casts a small ball, called the *cochonnet*, about twenty to thirty feet away. He then throws his first *boule* aiming to get as near the *cochonnet* as possible. Then his opponent tries, and whoever is nearest starts the game and throws all his *boules*. One favourite shot is the *tireur*, where the *boule* is thrown high in the air, with back spin, to drop on the opponent's *boule* and knock it away from the *cochonnet*. In a team game one team plays first, then the other, not the players alternately. The winning team scores one point for every *boule* they get nearer the *cochonnet*, than the best of the opposing team's *boules*. When all the *boules* have been thrown, the first player of the winning team draws a circle round the *cochonnet*, steps into it and starts again from there. The first team to score thirteen points wins.

The locals take it very seriously, and one player assured me that France intended to get *pétanque* included in the list of Olympic Games, which would, if it happened, ensure a certain Gold, Silver and Bronze Medal for France, which is probably the idea!

*   *   *

Florac is surrounded by the steep escarpments of the great Causses, and lies on the road north towards Mende, the capital of the Département of Lozère. From Florac though, we will turn south and west, to run between two of the Causses, down the Gorges of the River Tarn.

3

The Grandes Causses
and Gorges du Tarn

A notable physical feature in Southern France are the Causses. They fall into three main groups of which the middle group, the Minor Causses, lies in Quercy, to the east of the Dordogne. The two other groups, the Grandes and Petites, lie in Languedoc. From Florac one can travel down across the four *Grandes Causses,* which are the Causse de Sauveterre, the Causse Méjean, the Causse Noir and the Causse du Larzac. Near these last two, lie the *Petites Causses,* the Causse Bégon, the Causse de Campestre and the Causse de Blandas.

A *causse* is a plateau, and all these *causses* were created by volcanic action thousands of years ago in the region of the Massif Central. This forced up the level of the land, and altered the flow of the rivers, sending them south and west. The Causses are interesting to visit because they offer a wide variety of scenery, differing according to their respective heights, (which vary between two and a half thousand and four thousand feet) and the different rocks of which they are composed. Some are of chalk and limestone, others of dolomite. Whatever the material, all are soft, and the rivers have, through millions of years, cut deep and beautiful valleys into the plateau. All these Gorges are attractive and near Florac lies the most famous of them all, the Gorges du Tarn. The Tarn Gorge is over fifty miles long, and up to a mile wide, flanked by tall cliffs.

The Tarn rises on Mount Lozère and flows south-west towards Albi, and runs into the Causses above Florac, where it is joined by the Tarnon tributary. From there the river divides the Causse de Sauveterre from the Causse Méjean, and makes a deep and spectacular route across the country.

Heading north from Florac, one comes to the head of the Gorges at Ispagnac. These *ac* endings are of Roman origin, from the word *aqua* meaning water, and Ispagnac is a nice village, full of fruit trees with a twelfth-century church and a large and excellent 'camping' on the meadows by the river.

The Gorges du Tarn

A little further on, and to the left, lies the fourteenth-century village of Quézac, reached across an ancient stone bridge, also some six hundred years old.

The bridge was built by order of the saintly Pope Urban V to enable pilgrims to visit the sanctuary in Quézac. This is a fine Gothic church with Urban's arms carved on one of the pillars in the nave.

Quézac is a real old village, all gloom and narrow streets, and visited under a lowering sky it was somewhat forbidding. I had hardly returned to the car when sheets of rain swept down from the Causse, and fell with such force that the windscreen wipers could not cope with the water and I had to stop. Within minutes the road had become a river, while the Tarn below rose rapidly, the waters swiftly covering the gravel banks. These sudden storms, or 'orages', of rain and hail are a feature of the Causse climate, and should be viewed with some care. You are perfectly safe from lightning in a car, but it is impossible to drive in the heavy rain and you must be careful where you park. The rain washes stones off the cliffs, and the wind can tear branches off the trees, which can be dangerous. Seated safely under a stone wall, below a fruit tree which rained cherries on the roof of the

The Tarn near Quézac

car, I was able to reach out and grab a wet handful to eat, but when the rain stopped and I moved off again, the road was littered for miles with torn branches, mud, stones and rocks of all sizes. One of these, coming off a cliff and on to the roof or through the windscreen could have done a lot of damage. There were two more *'orages'* during the day and I stopped, very circumspectly, each time.

The Gorges du Tarn are deep and steep, the road having been hacked into the cliffs above the river and sometimes, to overcome some particular problem, a tunnel has been driven into an outcrop of rock to carry the road through. This all makes for an interesting drive with magnificient views over the river. Generally, in summer, the Tarn is a shallow mountain river hereabouts, with rocks and rapids alternating along the course.

Here and there, on the white water stretches, poles have been suspended over the river, for the Tarn is a great centre for canoeists who come from all over Europe to enjoy the thrill of descending the swift exciting stretches below the tall dark cliffs.

By mid-morning I had arrived in the lovely little town of Ste Enimie, where the Tarn turns south. The road here goes over another of these beautiful Languedoc bridges. One can turn off here and travel over the Causse de Sauveterre to Mende, or to the north-west to La Canourgue. Both roads run over the wild Causse and the quiet and solitude are unbelievable. The Causses great attraction lies in the green spaces, the clear skies and an absolute absence of noise. You can almost here the silence.

Ste Enimie, now a tourist centre for touring the Causses, was once the sanctuary of a Merovingian princess, Ste Enimie. Enimie was the sister of King Dagobert, who wished to marry her to one of his more turbulent vassals. Enimie, however, wished to become a nun and prayed to God fervently for some event to stop the nuptials. She got her wish in a most unpleasant fashion, when she was struck down with leprosy. This put a stop to the marriage, and Enimie prayed again, this time for a cure. One day an angel appeared to her and told her to go and bathe in the spring by the Tarn at Burle. She did so and her leprosy, which was probably a nervous eczema, promptly disappeared. However, when she left the spring to return home, it reappeared, and her future path lay clear before her. Enimie lived the rest of her life by the spring, devoting herself to good works and the building of a nunnery. It was at this spot that the little town of Ste Enimie presently grew up. The fountain of Burle is still there at the back of the town, as is the old nunnery.

Below Ste Enimie the fine fifteenth-century castle of La Caze stands beside the road. La Caze is now a hotel, and a good one, warranting a rosette in the Michelin guide, with a restaurant which serves excellent local specialities such as trout and fresh-water crayfish. The castle has an interesting history. It was built at the end of the fifteenth century by the Seigneur de Alamand, who, poor man, was blessed with eight children, but all daughters and all so beautiful that

The Tarn in summer

they were famed throughout France as the "Nymphs of the Tarn". Their portraits decorate a ceiling in the hotel, and beauty being a subjective matter, let us say merely that the girls had a certain rustic charm! Providing doweries for his eight girls ruined the Seigneur. He should have opened an hotel, for at present prices he would have quickly had his money back.

At La Maléne the Lords of Montesquiou lived until the Revolution. Nowadays their only remembrance here is a restaurant by the river. Otherwise the village makes a living from tourism and the sale of gloves. The centre for glove-making in France is at Millau at the foot of the Causse Noir. Local gloves are excellently made, the skins coming from sheep reared on the Causses. They are therefore of fine quality and make good presents or souvenirs.

Just below La Maléne, the Tarn Gorge gets even narrower, and the river enters the part known as *Les Detroits* or the Narrows. You can take a boat trip down the river here, over some three miles of rapids, and below the *Detroits* where the trip ends, were a dozen watermen waiting to take the boats back up-stream against the current, standing on the bank and each leaning on the symbol of his profession. Not an oar nowadays, however, as each was propped up on his own individual outboard motor!

The Cirque du Baumes, where the river turns south is ringed with high cliffs, stained blue and black by some mineral in the rock. From this point the fast road runs through tunnels and open stretches, until the Tarn joins with the River Jonte at Le Rozier.

*   *   *

The Jonte divides the Causse Méjean from the next Causse, the Causse Noir, and the Gorge de La Jonte, between the two, is an airy, open pass with the cliffs ablaze with wild flowers. After the enclosed Gorges of the Tarn, it is very pleasant to be out in the open again, with wonderful views to the high escarpments of the Causses, as you turn down to Meyrueis, at the foot of the Jonte canyon.

At Meyrueis, one can head out of the Gorges for a while, across the Causse Noir via Lanuejols, towards Montpellier le Vieux. The Causse Noir is much the smallest of the Grandes Causses, and, I think, the most pleasant. It takes its name from the dark pine forest that cloaks some of the hills. It is sheep country, with vast flocks

Sheep and 'sotch' on the Causse Noir

moved about by the shepherds and their dogs. It is difficult to write objectively about the Causses. There is nothing there, just open, sun-struck country, full of sheep and solitude. They are all very beautiful, and as a place to get away from crowds and just listen to the silence, they are quite perfect. After the clamour of the cities they are a bless-ing; but one must not be a bore. The Causses are quiet and empty. If you like solitude you will love them. Enough said! Sheep can graze, but the Causses support little other life, being so high and dry. Very little else can survive, and in winter the weather can be bitter. How-ever, here and there in little hollows, the rocks have been painfully cleared away, and the ground ploughed and planted. These little oases are called 'sotchs', and they make a pleasant green or gold patch on the barren, stoney ground.

From here the gourmet can veer off, out of Languedoc for a while, to visit the cheese caves at Roquefort, in Aveyron. Roquefort is a sharp, tangy cheese, which for some reason will only mature in the limestone caves behind the town. The cheese mine is a curious sight, hollowed out of the cliffs, and should not be willingly missed.

Alternatively, you can head across the Causse Noir, until you even-tually reach Montpellier-le-Vieux. Montpellier-le-Vieux isn't a place; it is an illusion, a *Chaos*. The wind and rain have carved the soft rock into weird shapes elsewhere in the Causses or the Cévennes, but in some places they seem to have created whole buildings and castles out of the rocks.

Such a place is Monpellier-le-Vieux, and it is quite an attractive spot, full of trees and flowers and the 'towers' and 'houses' of the *Chaos*. You have to leave the car some distance away from the site and walk, which can be hot work on a summer afternoon.

From here it is back, heading south again, down another deep valley, the Gorges de la Dourbie, through Nant, to the fascinating Commanderie of the Knights Templar at La Couvertoirade.

One of the side benefits of travel is that it reminds you that historical figures really existed, and that historical dramas happened, not in the pages of a book, but here, at this place, down that street, under this sun. It is fascinating to touch a wall, and know that a hand, like your own, placed it there hundreds of years ago.

Such a place, steeped in history, is La Couvertoirade, a small, walled town, a garrison and pilgrim station, dating from the twelfth century.

It should really be called a Preceptory, not a Commanderie. Here lived the local Commander, or Preceptor, of the Knights Templar. From this post, he administered the Templar houses in lower Languedoc, and when the Templars were extinguished, the town passed to the Knights of St John, who held it into the seventeenth century. It is quiet now, no commands are being barked on the parade ground by the castle, and no armoured horsemen ride through the gate to reach the jousting ground outside the walls. The Knights are long gone, but their former possessions still remain.

Many places in Languedoc were owned by the Knights, and since their foundations stud the pages of this book, it might be as well to know a little of their proud history and tragic end.

The order of the Poor Knights of the Temple of Jerusalem, or the Templars, as they were more usually called, was one of three great Military Orders which arose out of the Crusades. The first Order, that of St John, was originally devoted to the care of the sick, and they were usually called the Knights Hospitaller. The Temple was founded as a fighting Order of Soldier Monks dedicated to war against the Moslems. Their rules called for the observation of the precepts of chastity, poverty and obedience, and their first seal, to symbolise their poverty, showed two Knights riding one horse. The

Order was almost instantly successful and quickly prosperous. It was founded with only nine Knights in 1118, and after obtaining their Rule and Papal recognition in 1128, they quickly gained recruits and, more significantly, grants of land and money poured in from all over Europe. One King of Aragon left the Templars a third of his kingdom in his will and only the fierce defiance of his countrymen prevented the Order claiming it. No more than ten percent of the Templars were Knights, for most Templars were merely Sergeants, but all swore the same vows, and entry to the Order was made extremely difficult. The Templars, soon joined by warriors from their rival Order of St John, fought in all the Crusades, and were the bastion of Outremer against the Saracen. It should be remembered that although there were many major Crusades, not every year brought a General Passage, when the Kings of Christendom flocked to defend the Holy Places. These major campaigns were rare events and, for the most part, the defence of Outremer depended on men recruited for, and trained by, the Military Orders.

'As the years passed and their power grew, the Templars adopted another, fatal, function. With Commanderies everywhere, good aris-

La Couvertoirade, the Château

tocratic connections, and a reputation for honesty, they became bankers. Medieval money was usually in silver pennies, heavy to carry, easy to detect and steal. How much easier to pay in money to the Templars in Paris, and draw out the balance in Jerusalem, obtaining travelling expenses against the draft from Templar outposts on the way. The Templars were popular stake-holders in the Middle Ages, having the power to hold whatever they held in trust, and the honesty to return it when the time was due.

In their white cloaks, with the red cross of Jerusalem on the shoulder, they must have been a familiar sight in the thirteenth century, as more and more men were recruited to head east and fight and die for Christendom against the tide of Islam.

But for all this the Templars were not popular. They were too rich, too successful, above the law, owing allegiance to none save the Pope, and eventually in 1291, when the Kingdom of Jerusalem finally fell, the Templars received a large and unjustified share of the blame. The Grand Master of the Order, Jacques de Molay, retired to Cyprus with less than two hundred Templars, taking with him the vast treasure of the Order. That treasure was to bring about the downfall of the Templars.

Primarily the Order was French. There were Templars of every nation, but the bulk were French. So, too, was their most deadly enemy, Philip the Fair, King of France, and worse, he had the first Avignon Pope, Clement V, in his pocket.

It is still not clear why Philip detested the Templars. That he wanted their money is understandable, as they had lots of it and he was permanently hard up. But he moved against them so relentlessly and organized his attack so successfully, that some other motive seems to lie behind his enmity. He was neurotic, always nervous of any threat to his authority, and the Templars were outside his control; another man's private army, within his own Kingdom. Perhaps this frightened him.

Whatever the reason, he resolved on their disgrace and ruin. In 1306 he ordered the Pope, Clement V, to summon the Grand Master to France, intending to destroy him. All unsuspecting, Jacques de Molay obeyed.

When he arrived in France he heard slanders everywhere against the Templars. They were accused of heresy, unnatural vice, disgusting initiation practices, of treachery to the West and of plotting against the life and throne of the French King. Aghast at these stories, de Molay saw the King and the Pope, and asked for an official enquiry to clear the charges rumoured against the Order. His reception was very favourable, and he took up residence at the Temple in Paris, to await the hearing.

Philip's next move was organized with great care and discretion. On the night of Friday 13th October 1306, every Commanderie in France was raided, and all the Templars were arrested. None offered any resistance. Jacques de Molay and sixty of his Knights were taken from the Temple in Paris to prison and handed over to the torturers. Philip wanted confessions, and every device was employed to see he got them.

He accused the Templars specifically of blasphemy and homosexuality. The Knights were told that, if and when they confessed, their tortures would stop. Eventually, under rack and fire, they began to do so. Many held out, expecting their overlord, the Pope, to intervene, but he was Philip's creature, and merely added his exhortation to confess, to those of their present tormentors.

What follows is nowadays a familiar story, after the days of Hitler and Stalin. Knight after Knight appeared before the Inquisition in Paris and confessed to crimes and vices they had never committed, implicating others as they did so. Trials of Templars took place all over France, at Beaucaire, Aigues Mortes, Nîmes, Avignon and Carcassonne.

While all this was going on, Philip kept France quiet with bribes, promising his nobles, many of whom had relatives in the Order, a share in their wealth and lands; with lies, in which the Church supported him, the priests slandering the Order from the pulpit; and with subtle threats. If the King could overwhelm a mighty organization like the Temple, who was safe?

The trials against the Templars went on for years, in France and elsewhere. Philip had sent copies of his charges to his fellow Kings in Europe, and the Order was suppressed everywhere, usually without bloodshed, many of the Templars simply joining the Knights Hospitaller of St. John, by then established in Rhodes.

In France though, the persecution continued, and the Order was ruthlessly suppressed. Finally, in 1314, after years in prison, the Grand Master, Jacques de Molay, and the Preceptor of the Order, Geoffrey de Charney, were brought before the Cathedral of Notre Dame, and having confessed, recanted and re-confessed, were sentenced, as an act of mercy, to perpetual imprisonment. At this, at last, out in the open, before a crowd of people, de Molay spoke the truth, in such a manner that none could doubt it.

"I declare that the Order is innocent of all crimes and blasphemies. To what we have confessed is a lie, said to destroy us, and admitted by torture, and fear of torture. We have said, by torture, what our enemies wished us to say, and death is not so awful, that we must, for fear of it, admit to foul crimes we have never committed. If the price of life is paid in infamy, I will not pay it, for at such a price life is not worth having."

De Charney then spoke his mind, and the prisoners were hustled away through a shocked and murmuring throng. Next day, the prisoners were brought again before Notre Dame, where the stake and faggots for burning awaited them. History tells that Philip was present at the execution, and that as de Molay became engulfed in the flames, he cried out, "Clement, false Pope and perjurer. I summon you before the Tribunal of God in thirty days, and you, Philip, within one year."

Clement was dead within the month, and Philip died nine months later.

*   *   *

This then is the brief history of the Templars. In Languedoc they guarded the pilgrimage routes, especially the one to Compostella, and the visitor will therefore see Templar houses in many towns.

La Couvertoirade was built by the Templars in the twelfth century. From the Commanderies the local lands of the Order were administered, and recruits to the Order were trained in arms and in warfare against the Moslems, before being sent to Outremer. La Couvertoirade was also used as a hospital and retirement centre for old or sick Templars, who could pass on their experience to the younger Knights and Sergeants. When the Knights of St. John took over La Couvertoirade they maintained it as a hospital for pilgrims.

The village is completely walled, and it is possible to climb up and walk around on the ramparts. The castle in one corner dates from the

The rooftops of La Couvertoirade

twelfth century, as does the Templar Church, and both are now being restored.

Most of the houses within the walls date from the sixteenth century, and were built by the Hospitallers. Nowadays, an attempt is being made to bring life back to La Couvertoirade with the establishment of a craft centre. There is a weaving shed and a pottery, with various other shops and galleries. Outside the walls is a *lavogne*, a dew pond, built to water the horses and livestock of the Knights, and now used to supply the local flocks of sheep. There is little running water up here on the Causse, and *lavognes* are quite common, especially around Roquefort, where the cheese comes from.

Scores of sheep were moving towards the *lavogne* at La Couvertoirade as the evening came on, their myriad bells tinkling together to make a great din.

"Listen to the muttons", the lady in the cafe said to me, in a gallant stab at English. "They are our lives here." We went outside and listened to the muttons. It didn't sound a bit like the jingle of spurs and knightly armour, but that, nowadays, is how the little town lives.

4

Navacelles to Nîmes

There can be few things as refreshing after a heavy night, as a large cup of café-au-lait, with a hot *croissant.* Unless it be two large cups! On this particular morning, sitting on the sunny terrace of the Auberge du Cascade at the very bottom of the Cirque de Navacelles, two seemed especially welcome.

The café and the *croissant* seemed so typically French, and so much a part of the day there, that it is curious to reflect that the *croissant* did not originate in France at all, but began, quite romantically, in Vienna.

In the mid-seventeenth century, when the Turks invaded Europe, all fell down before them, until they laid siege to Vienna. After some months of siege, the inhabitants of the city were on very short rations indeed, and one baker, admittedly a Frenchman, when racking his brains for a way to eke out his meagre allowance of flour and fat, struck on the idea of making it into rolls, shaped like the Turkish emblem of the crescent, which he and all the other citizens saw daily, clustered round the walls.

The rolls were duly baked and put on display, and the patriot could actually devour, with relish, the enemy's symbol. Their popularity was assured and the baker's fortune was made. His 'crescents', or *croissants,* should have made his name a byword, but since his name is unknown and his idea long forgotten, perhaps it is just a story after all!

Navacelles ought to be famous too. The Cirque de Navacelles is an enormous ravine, circular in shape, about a mile across, and half a mile deep. It was carved out, down millions of years, by the River Vis which still bubbles clearly along the floor of the valley, and tumbles delightfully in a waterfall by the only public building in the village of Navacelles, the Auberge de la Cascade, the present owner of which, Gervais Vernay, should be remembered also, for he is trying and succeeding in a difficult task. He wants to save his birthplace from extinction.

A misty view down into Navacelles

Much of rural France is becoming depopulated. Along the gorges and on the Causses, there are scores of ruined houses and many abandoned villages. The young people will just not live there any more and, as the older people die, life is gradually extinguished. Without Gervais Vernay, Navacelles would already have joined this collection. In spite of the unique beauty of the sight, Navacelles was dying. The permanent population even today, is only fifteen people, and when his daughter was born five years ago, she was the first child born in the village for twenty-five years. Gervais Vernay was born in Navacelles and loves the place. He decided, rightly, that a community of fiteen people could never be economic and a passing trade was vital. He decided to build an hotel. It must have taken rare pluck to invest time and savings in an hotel at the bottom of a pit in the middle of nowhere, yet that is what he did.

Navacelles is beautiful, but it is very remote and difficult to get to. Gervais Vernay decided that these facts were assets, and time has proved him right. The very remoteness, the feeling of an enclosed community at Navacelles is immensely attractive. It is the sort of place you leave vowing to return to often. And many people do.

Among fellow guests were a Belgian couple who had stayed at the hotel over Christmas in 1970, when a rare and unexpected blizzard swept off the Causse and snowed them in for twelve days. All the guests had to rally round to cut firewood and keep things going, and at night they gathered round in blankets and kept close to the fire. Everyone seems to have had a high old time, and when the road at last opened they departed with reluctance.

Over the years the Auberge has been extended, although it still has only six bedrooms, but it has all amenities, laboriously installed by Gervais Vernay, the cooking is excellent and the wines well chosen; all matched by the hospitality, which brought me next day to the terrace, with a slight headache and a craving for coffee.

In the Middle Ages, Navacelles contained a religious community. Monks came here for retreat and contemplation. English soldiers also arrived, during the Hundred Years War, and they built the beautiful and delicate bridge which spans the Vis just above the village. It is a pack-horse bridge, not wide enough for carts, and with shallow parapets.

The Vis, and the waterfall, make the place delightful. The water is warm and shallow, crystal clear over the gravel and tumbling down in a white sheet just by the hotel. In Navacelles the sound of water is everywhere.

Navacelles is too small, thank goodness, ever to be commercialised, and will, I hope, remain a place to remember and visit for many years to come.

*   *   *

It took about twenty minutes driving, with the wheel usually locked fully over, to climb up from the bottom of the Cirque. The air was clear, and smelling of honeysuckle. Once out of the Cirque, the road to Ganges and the Grotte des Demoiselles runs through trees along the banks of the Vis, which is a lovely river, spurting over rocks and rapids until it runs into the Hérault at Ganges. The Hérault gives its name to the Département, and thus marks the point at which, for the first time in days, we emerge from the mountains and seek a change of pace and scene on the coastal plain. First, though, a little side trip to the underground caves of the Grotte des Demoiselles.

The Cascade in Navacelles

14th century Packhorse bridge, Navacelles

Huge underground caves are very common in the limestone causse country. The rock is porous and soft so that water can collect underground and hollow out caves and tunnels as it presses its way through the rock. In the resulting caverns, stalactites form and, with a little use of imagination, these can be seen to resemble men, or houses, or, as in the present case, the Virgin and Child, from which the Grotte des Demoiselles is named. Floodlit with coloured lights, these caverns make an interesting excursion, and as the Demoiselle is the best known, it may serve as an example for the rest. It lies near Ganges, up on the side of the plateau, and from the terraces you have fine views over Hérault to the mountains of the Serraine.

The tour starts every fifteen minutes, and lasts about an hour. You enter the Grotto by a railway which takes you some two hundred yards into the hill, from which you have a guided tour to the various sites. It is an interesting trip, but a trifle chilly. I must remember to wear a sweater next time!

Among the other caverns in the area, are the Grotto de Clamouse, near Montpellier, Trabuc, near Alès, Bramabiau, near Meyrueis, and the Aven Armand, south of the Gorges du Tarn. These are the main ones and there are many more.

Emerging again into the warmth of the sunshine, it seemed a good idea to picnic on the banks of the Hérault. Below Laroque the banks are wide and empty and, sheltered from the wind, it is possible to cool off a bottle of wine in the river, and improve the suntan.

The *Occitans,* as the people who live in the Languedoc are called, enjoy, or suffer from, a variety of winds which have impressed the locals to the extent that most of them have names.

There is the *mistral,* a cold buffeting wind that roars down the Rhône Valley. On the Causses there is the *Autun,* a dry wind, while off the sea comes the *Marin.* From the Pyrénées comes the *Tratamontane.* Then there is the *Grec.* On the day I arrived at Nîmes a gale was blowing across the plain, but this was only the *Vent du Nord,* the north wind, not worthy of special designation, although it seemed strong enough to me.

Heading south from Ganges, the road comes to the little village of St. Martin de Londres, which calls itself the capital of the *garrigue.* Garrigue is heathland, the tree-less, stoney, gorse country, covered with scrub which is a paradise for sheep. Rain on the garrigue is delightful for it brings out the scent of the gorse. St. Martin has a better claim for attention than many more famous places, in the beautiful Romanesque church and cloisters situated in the middle of the town. The name, incidentally, has nothing to do with London, but is a corruption of the name *lutrine,* or otter, as otters were once very common hereabouts.

The church is a perfect example of the Romanesque, and has a host of interesting features. To the right of the door a mass dial is grooved into the stone. Mass dials were primitive sundials, used by the priest to tell him the hours of mass, so that he knew when to toll the church bell and summon the congregation. On the left, built into the stone is a rich man's stone coffin lid. It has to belong to a rich man for poor men had no coffins!

There is a statue of what appears to be a mounted knight on the tympanum arch, and inside the door, a small bishop blesses the visitor from a niche in the walls. On the stone pulpit, dated seventeenth century, but I believe earlier, are coats of arms and cherubim. All in all, a delightful little church.

Leaving St. Martin and heading east, the road runs across the *gar-*

rigue, through clear, open country, through the pass below the shadow of the towering Pic de St.-Loup. On either crest of the Pass lie ruined castles, once, as one might guess, the strongholds of the local robber barons. These castles, like so many others in Languedoc, were destroyed by the orders of Richelieu. We shall be discussing the great Cardinal later, but one of his policies which failed to have the effect he intended, or rather had an unfortuante effect subsequently, was his intention to destroy the military power of the nobility and ensure the dominance of his King, Louis XIII. He made the nobility dependent on the King when he broke their power, dispersed their followers, and destroyed their strongholds. It took a little time, and Louis XIV had the Fronde Wars to contend with at the start of his reign, but in the end the nobles had no work to do, except to stay at Versailles where they could gawp at the Sun King and he, in turn, could keep an eye on them.

He did, too! Louis XIV had a fantastic memory, and if he failed to glimpse one of his nobles, when parading in to dinner, the wretch having gone home or, worse still, to Paris, the King would intone, "I do not see him", and trouble followed. To keep the nobles amused, Louis tried to give them all little tasks, like handing him his shirt, or polishing the royal apple, but while all this was very nice, the people, who had at least known their lords in the old days, even if they did not particularly like them, now grew apart from them and, neglected in their misery, matured for the eventual Revolution which came, not from the nobility as Richelieu had feared, but against them.

South of the Pic St.-Loup, lies the town of Castries, which has a large, red-roofed château, modestly described as the 'Versailles of the Midi', a title contested by quite a number of other castles in Languedoc.

The château was built in the sixteenth century, with later additions, and is full of interesting exhibits. It is open to the public in the summer, every day except Monday. The most striking feature in the town is the aqueduct which stretches away from the town towards the north. This was built by Paul Riquet, who constructed the Canal du Midi, in the seventeenth century and, although long disused, it makes a pleasant feature running across the landscape.

After Castries there is a choice of route for Nîmes. One can go either by the recently completed Auto-route, or along the coastal road. I chose the latter, passing through Lunel.

After the quiet countryside and roads of the Causses and

The Maison Carrée at Nîmes

Cévennes, the volume of traffic by the coast was shattering. The littoral is being rapidly developed into an industrial and tourist area—the two aims being not entirely exclusive, and the roads in summer are full of foreign cars and caravans, in addition to the normal commercial traffic. The road runs through endless vineyards, which cover most of Hérault, and the coastal plain generally. Nîmes was a Roman city, the finest in Southern France, and remains proud of the connection to this very day. In the Maison Carrée, it possesses the finest example of a Roman temple, although the lines are Greek in the Corinthian style. It was built by Greek craftsmen in honour of the grandsons of the Emperor Augustus, and stands on the site of the old Forum, the centrepiece of Roman civic life. Nearby is the Arena, again virtually complete, which can seat twenty thousand people and is still used for games and bullfights during the annual Fiesta.

In pre-Roman times, Nîmes was the site of a spring sacred to the Gauls. It fell to the Romans in the first century B.C. and, as was usual in the days of the Republic, retired legionaries were given grants of land there and encouraged to marry local girls. After the Antonine Wars, legionaries from Egypt were settled there and the Egyptian connection is well maintained by the town's arms which show the chained crocodile of the Nile, and a palm tree. In the fifth century, with the collapse of the Empire, the city fell to the Vandals, and later, like the rest of Southern Gaul, to the Visigoths, who added towers to the Arena, and used it as a fort. Indeed, the Arena has been in some sort of occupancy for most of its existence. In the Middle Ages it was a village, and in Napoleonic times, a barracks.

Apart from the Roman remains, which are seen and stressed everywhere, Nîmes is a lively, bustling city, rather too full of cars, with excellent shops and restaurants. It runs a very full programme of artistic events, and holds regular festivals of music, and dancing. Over what used to be the Whitsun weekend, six weeks after Easter, the town holds its great festival. The Grande Fiesta, with bullfighting and shows in the Arena, goes on over the four days of the weekend. Even during a normal week in summer, there are special events. On Mondays, for example, there is a wine market along the main street, the Avenue Victor Hugo, where excellent wines can be sampled and purchased at reasonable prices. These many attractions bring thousands of visitors to Nîmes every summer, and the tourist would be well advised to either book before going, or find a hotel room early in the day. After five o'clock in the evening, it gets more difficult by the minute. Whatever modern attractions the city strives to offer, most people who come to Nîmes, come to see the Roman remains, the best preserved of any in the Mediterranean. They are in good condition because wherever possible they have remained in use. The uses of the Arena have already been mentioned, and the Maison Carrée, has had many uses down the centuries also, serving once as the Town Hall. It is now a museum.

The Roman baths in what is now the Jardin de la Fontaine, were transformed into attractive gardens in the seventeenth century. The old sacred spring is still here, and the Roman watchtower, the Tour Magne, once part of the defensive walls, stands above the gardens and can be climbed for beautiful views over the city.

Many people go from Nîmes to visit the Pont du Gard, which we visited earlier. It is not far away and was designed to carry water as part of an aqueduct, into Nîmes from a spring at Uzès, which is thirty miles outside the city.

As the visitor will quickly learn, Nîmes takes a great pride in being the 'Rome of France', and treasures the ancient connections with those good old Imperial Days. This is understandable, if a little tiresome, for the town has one or two other claims to our attention.

It is, for example, the birthplace of the writer Alphonse Daudet, who was born in 1840 in the Rue Gambetta, and he is commemorated in various ways all over the town.

Unfortunately, he took himself off to Provence to write his *Letters de Mon Moulin* and the best that Nîmes can do is organise coach trips to his windmill, which is near Les Baux on the 'wrong' side of the Rhône. Daudet's play *L'Arlesienne* was the inspiration for Bizet's music, and this celebrated piece about the girls of Arles gybes with Nîmes' claim to have the most beautiful girls in France, which a tour of the town would appear to substantiate!

Perhaps it is the presence of the nearby Camargue, or the relaxed style of the local people, but the rather stiff attitudes of provincial France seem a little less noticeable here. Nîmes seems to have her roots in Rome, and her heart elsewhere.

A little south of Nîmes lies the little town of St. Gilles, today small and neglected, but once one of the most important pilgrimage centres between Rome and Compostella. It contains still the tomb of St. Gilles, and was a favourite foundation of the Counts of Toulouse, one of whom, Raymond de St. Gilles, led the Languedoc contingent to Jerusalem in the First Crusade. At St Gilles, in 1208, a squire of Raymond, Count of Toulouse, slew the Papal Legate, Pierre de Castelnau, after a quarrel, and gave Pope Innocent III, the excuse he needed to begin the Albigensian Crusade. To save his lands and title, Raymond submitted to the Pope and later, as a penance, was publically flogged before the altar in the Church of St. Gilles. The front of the church is now badly defaced, and the whole building suffered considerably during the Wars of Religion.

From Nîmes, one can make excursions to the Camargue, which, although it lies across the Petit Rhône and outside the scope of this book, is so near to the border that it cannot be neglected.

The Camargue lies in a vast triangle between the two arms of the Rhône, an area of shallow lakes, scrub and salt-flats, a paradise for birdlife and home of a race of fine black bulls, herded by their *guardiens* on white horses. The *guardiens* are the local cowboys and look, like the Spanish *vaquero*, as if they had just slipped out of a Western film. Their equipment and saddles strike the same note, but the bulls are controlled, not with the lasso, but with a short lance equipped with a blunt crescent-shaped head. Their beautiful white ponies are bred in the Camargue, and supposedly descend from Arab horses brought to the region by the Saracens.

The *guardiens* are also great experts in the local bullfights. The traveller in Languedoc-Roussillon will, during the summer, see many posters advertising bullfights. The Spanish influence has lapped over the province, and some of these fights are the genuine Spanish *corrida* with matadors, ending in the death of the bull.

More popular, especially with the young bloods of the region, is the Languedocian version, the *cours libre*. In this, the bull, usually the small, nimble Camargue beast, is not killed, the object being to remove rosettes and tassels from between his horns while the bull, naturally enough, tries to flatten his tormentors against the nearest wall. This sport is quite bloodless, certainly as far as the bull is concerned, and the men involved, the *razateurs* come off, at worst, with little more than a cracked rib. Either way, to watch man and bull chasing each other about, each relying on speed and agility to score off the other, is great fun and popular with both tourist and local.

Whatever their background, the *guardiens*, pursuing an old craft in the old manner, are a real glimpse into the past, although one that is rapidly fading. Although now declared a National Park, the fringes of the Camargue contain a number of holiday ranches, where the *guardiens* are employed in taking tourists on horseback rides into the marshes, acquiring, one gathers, the sort of formidable reputation with the ladies formerly reserved for beach guards and ski-instructors!

The centre of the Camargue is a wildlife sanctuary, where only accredited naturalists are admitted to study the wild fowl, and in particular, the beautiful flamingoes of the region.

Also in the Camargue lies the little town and holiday resort of the Saintes Maries de la Mer, where so legend had it, Marie, mother of the Apostles James and John; Mary, sister of Lazarus; and Mary Magdalene, and their servant Sarah all arrived in a boat, having fled persecution in the Holy Land following the Crucifixion. A church was built on the spot where they landed, and the place has been a pilgrimage centre since the Middle Ages, and still is, especially for gypsies. Gypsies come from all over Europe, to be at Les Saintes Maries on the feast day of Saint Sara, the Egyptian servant, on the 24th May. European gypsies claim to have come from Egypt originally, hence their name, and the festival of Ste Sara is the event of the year in the Camargue. Secular travellers will find the Stes Marie strangely familiar, until, on the beach, this sense of *déja vu* is explained by seeing the boats drawn up on the sand, when memory floods back, for these are the very boats which Van Gogh painted hereabouts, and they are, it is said, just like the boat that brought the Saints ashore here nearly two thousand years ago.

5

Aigues-Mortes, Montpellier and St Guilhem

Few towns in the world smack so much of the Middle Ages as Aigues-Mortes. This, the city of the 'Dead Waters' was established by the French Crusader King, Louis IX and developed and fortified by his son, Philip the Bold, and his grandson, Philip the Fair.

When St Louis decided to fulfill a lifetime's vow and ambition, by leading a General Passage to the Holy Land, he was faced at once with a major problem; he had no port at which to embark his army. By the middle of the thirteenth century the Crusading expeditions had made themselves mighty unwelcome in the lands of the Holy Roman Empire and Byzantium, through which they had to pass to reach Outremer. Most Pilgrims, therefore, went by sea, from Italy, but Louis was on bad terms with the Empire, and decided to build a port of his own.

He purchased Aigues-Mortes from its owners, the monks of Psalmody. They had a little industry here, collecting salt from the marshes, but it was a fever ridden spot, and they were glad to hand it over for a good price. Louis built the Tower de Constance, and had a channel or *grau* dug across the marshes to connect Aigues-Mortes with the sea. From here, in 1248, he sailed with an army of fifteen thousand men, which included strong contingents from the Hospital and Temple, and landed and captured Damietta in Egypt. Then, when he had all but defeated the Egyptian army at Mansourah, the impetuosity of the Military Orders led his army to ruin. The Christians were totally defeated, and Louis and many of his Knights were taken prisoner.

Thousands of the foot soldiers and all the Knights of the Hospital and Temple were executed by their captors. Louis was later ransomed by his wife, and returned to France a chastened man. However, he regarded his crusading vow as unfulfilled and in 1270, when an old man, he led an army out of France, again through Aigues-Mortes, and laid siege to Tunis. There he died, his vow still unfulfilled, in the autumn of the same year.

Aigues-Mortes is picturesque because, unlike most medieval cities, it has not been greatly restored, and later development has kept away from outside the ancient walls. Except for around the Tour de Constance which stands outside the city by the main gate, the moat has been filled in, and the area outside the walls to the south is used for sport and fairs. Inside, the town is unremarkable, except for the main square, which contains a fine statue of St Louis, set above a fountain. The town is a great tourist attraction, and attracts many visitors, who tour the walls and inspect the carvings in the Tour de Constance. This great building, a hundred feet high, with walls twenty feet thick, was built by St Louis to protect the workers during the construction of the town. It lies outside the main *enciente*, and is connected with the walls by a narrow bridge which spans the only part of the original moat left undrained. It was a prison for centuries. The Templars were kept here, awaiting trial and torture, and when, in the fifteenth century, Burgundian allies of the English King, Henry V, took the town, they locked up the remains of the garrison here. During the Wars of Religion it held Huguenot prisoners.

Later, and a far worse story, is that after the Revocation of the Edict of Nantes by Louis XIV, which led to the Camisard Revolt, the wives and children of the Camisards were held here, in particular one little girl, Marie Durand, who was put into the tower at the age of eight and kept there for forty years! When she was released, as a middle-aged woman, in 1767, it was done as an act of clemency, although exactly what crime an eight year old child could commit that required the Royal 'clemency' has never been explained.

On a lighter note, the town has several comfortable hotels, and pleasant restaurants in one of which, the Au Camargue, gypsy guitarists from the Camargue play some wonderful music. You will have plenty of time to listen, for it is the only restaurant I have ever visited where you can go out for a stroll between courses.

Leaving Aigues-Mortes for the Grau du Roi, you will pass, on the left, the salt pans of the Salins du Midi. From about June until September the water in the pans is a most remarkable purple colour, which is caused by the action of the sun on the salt.

The process of salt collection starts in May, when the pans are filled with sea water. As this water evaporates, more sea water is added so that, by degrees, the salinity of the water is increased. As it does so the colour of the water changes to purple and deep mauve. This process is contained until the end of September, when complete

The Tour de Constance, Aigues-Mortes

evaporation leaves piles of salt to be collected, amounting to some five hundred thousand tons annually. A great white salt mountain stands behind the purple waters, ready for refining, and distribution all over France.

Salt has been collected here since the time of St. Louis, for in medieval times salt was just about the only seasoning and preservative available. The process of distillation has not changed.

The Grau du Roi is a pleasant port, but an indifferent beach resort, from which the road leads on to the remarkable pyramids and ziggurats of the newest, new town in the Languedoc littoral, La Grande Motte. There is not a great deal to be said about the place; it has to be seen. Modern architecture is usually bland and unimaginative, two charges that cannot be levelled against La Grande Motte.

Personally, I like it. It has wide streets, shady arcades, excellent shops and restaurants, a magnificent marina for over two thousand boats, and fine, clean beaches. Also, dazzling in the sunlight, it looks good. Whether, in a hundred years time it will please the eye, remains to be seen, but on balance, it has a twenty-first century look already.

The walls of Aigues-Mortes

La Grande Motte

There are half a dozen of these new resort towns on the coast between the Rhône and the Pyrénées, all well worth a visit.

*   *   *

Between the beach resort of Carnon-Plage and Montpellier, the road runs past the airport. Between the road and the runways, a huge flock of flamingoes waded in the shallow waters of the *étang*, taking off for brief flights around the lake. This is unusual, for naturalists believe that flamingoes are disturbed by aircraft noise. If this is so, these birds seem unaware of it. Flamingoes are a protected bird in the Midi, and the pride of the Camargue. It was nice to see them here, going about their own affairs right in the middle of a commercial centre. Scores of cars were pulling up, the passengers emerging with cameras and binoculars, to give some evidence of the present genera-tion's ever-growing interest in wildlife. The birds were more white

73

than pink, with that flowing flash of colour only visible on the outspread wing as they took off, or sailed in to splash down in the shallow water.

Flamingoes are not naturally pink. The colour is a glandular secretion due to their staple diet of small shrimps. If the shrimps cannot be found, the birds survive well enough, but they lose their colour. Perhaps the growing pollution of the local waters is killing off their natural food source. Obtaining shrimps to keep their flamingoes pink was a problem that worried zoo-keepers for years until, quite recently, a substitute was discovered which the birds would eat, and which kept them rosy.

*   *   *

Montpellier is the capital of Bas-Languedoc and of the *département* of Hérault. It is a large town of over a hundred and fifty thousand people, and like all large towns is locked in combat with the motor

The pyramid apartments of La Grande Motte

car, which is regrettably winning. The Place de La Comedie, once nicknamed 'The Egg', where the students from the University used to gather, is being uprooted to make a huge underground car park, and the city is now ringed with freeways and flyovers. The din is terrible.

From the centre you should take a stroll through the narrow lanes of the old part of the town, the *Quartier de L'Ancien Courrier*. This area is full of little cafés, boutiques, fine shops, bars and workshops, and makes a most interesting route through the heart of the town to the University and the Cathedral of St Pierre.

At one point, opposite another Templar Commanderie, you can see the house where James I of Aragon was born. Montpellier was a Spanish town and formed, for a while after 1262, part of the short-lived Kingdom of Majorca, which comprised the Balearics, Roussillon, and the fief of Montpellier. Montpellier was sold to the King of France in 1349. The town was almost completely destroyed in the Wars of Religion.

The University, with over thirty thousand students, is the heart of the town's life, and is both large and ancient, being, after the Sorbonne, the second oldest university in France, dating from the thirteenth century. It was, like all medieval universities, run by the clergy, and the Faculty of Medicine, where Rabelais studied, is joined on to the monstrous Cathedral. It was while he was studying at Montpellier between 1530 and 1538 that Rabelais wrote his *Pantagruel* and, later, his *Gargantua*. The students of Montpellier are still a lively crowd, much given to roaring about on motor-bicycles. Hell hath no fury like a student on a scooter, and crossing the road in Montpellier can be a hazardous task, but a visit should be made to the Aqueduct, which was built in the eighteenth century to bring water from St Clement and the Promenade de Peyrou. The artistic joy of Montpellier is the Musée Fabre, an art gallery founded in the late eighteenth century by Xavier Fabre, a disciple of David. It contains both paintings and sculpture of the French, Dutch and Spanish schools.

*   *   *

The wines of Languedoc-Roussillon are of great variety, and little reputation. This last is a pity for the wines generally are very good

In the Quartier de L'Ancien Courrier, Montpellier

and improving all the time. Languedoc is the largest wine producing area in France, both in area and for volume of production. Séte is the largest wine port in France, exporting millions of gallons and, to the occasional fury of the locals, importing considerable quantities from Italy and Algeria. The Algerian imports are especially galling for many of the local vignerons are Frenchmen, the so-called *pied-noirs*, who were driven from their vineyards in Algeria after Independence. Here, in Languedoc, they started again, and with a replanting programme, financed with government aid, they have greatly improved the quality of the local product. Previously, Languedoc wines had been used as the cheap house wines of Northern restaurants and cafés, and for the rough *pinard*, the staple drink of the French infantry soldier.

Much of the wine, blended with the Italian and Algerian imports, still fills such a purpose, and a good deal of mixing goes on, to produce a common or garden red, white or rosé, but increasingly the local wine is being marketed under identifiable names, with reliable quality controls. The manager of the Syndicat in Agde, which has a tasting centre for wine, told me proudly that while other wine regions have three types of wine, Languedoc has four; red, white, rosé, and gris-de-gris.

The largest producer of local wines is the Listel Company, Les Vins du Sable, who produce my favourite, the Listel *Gris-de-Gris,* a dry rosé, delicious with practically everything. *Gris* wines are so called because they leave a trace of grey sediment in the bottle. They are dry rosé wines, best when served chilled. Listel also produce a sound red and a good normal, slightly less dry, rosé, and an excellent Blanc de Blanc, all in distinctive bottles. Listel has a huge bottling plant just south of the Salins du Midi, which it also owns. Visitors are very welcome to look around and sample the local wine, and over twenty thousand people do so every year. Local wine is also on offer in the Syndicat in Aigues-Mortes and at Cap d'Agde and the numerous '*degustation*' or tasting stations along the roads. Don't be afraid to pull up and try a range of wines at these centres. That is what they are for, and you will be very welcome, especially if you buy a bottle to take away!

The visitor will find all the local wines very cheap, even the best, like the *Gris-de-Gris,* costing no more than Fr.6 a bottle, currently about 78p. Wines from the local co-operatives are even cheaper at Fr.2 to Fr.3 a bottle. These prices will obviously increase during the period this book is in print, but as some indication of value these prices will provide a guide.

In an area with so much wine, even generalisations can only skate over the surface. The *Gris-de-Gris* dry rosé wines are peculiar to the region. Also grown locally is Muscat, a sweet dessert wine named from the grape, and found around Lunel. From another type of grape, the Clairette, comes a medium sweet white wine, Clairmoel, while for a good dry white, Picpoul de Pinets Blanc-de-Blanc is excellent. Red wines, of VDQS standard from Hérault include Chateau Beaulieu and Saint Ohinian. Most Hérault wines are of VDQS grade.

Further south, the wines of the Corbières near Narbonne, and the reds from the Minervois by Carcassonne are very acceptable, while in the Roussillon is a further range of wines peculiar to the region, notably the dessert wine of Banyuls, and the excellent red Côtes de Roussillon. The great party wine in the south of Languedoc is the Blanquette de Limoux, a sparkling dry white wine, which comes from the countryside south of Carcassonne.

The visitor will note the local distribution of the wine. In any size of village, the local vintage is prominently featured on the wine list, and indeed wines from the local co-operative are frequently best, if bought locally and drunk at once. House wines are usually served in a *pichet*, a small jug.

Travelling across Languedoc-Roussillon, therefore, can be a real pleasure for the wine lover, for there is, quite literally, a different wine to be tried, every few miles.

Leaving Montpellier by the Lodève road, we go via Gignac, to reach another underground cave, the Grotto de Clamouse, and the Pont de Daible, built in the eleventh century, which spans the Hérault by St Jean de Fos. Two bridges span the river here, and the lower one is the old Pont. This is a beautiful spot, with waterfalls pouring down the gorge, and the river winding out into sandbanks and shallow rapids. Scores of people come here on hot afternoons or in the cool of the evening, to swim in the shallows, or paddle boats up the gorge to the waterfalls. Here too, the road bears off to run alongside the Hérault, up to the quaint village of St-Guilhem-le-Désert.

St Guilhem was a knight, a paladin of Charlemagne and noted for his skill at arms, his piety, and his short nose. While Guilhem was away at the wars, Charlemagne died and his son Louis came to the throne, and had distributed most of the available estates to others

The Gorge de Hérault at St Jean de Fos

before Guilhem returned. Guilhem was more than a little put out to find the coffers empty, and no reward awaiting his labours. Louis, who was fond of Guilhem, offered him various lands, all of which Guilhem, for one reason or another, refused. Finally, in despair, Louis suggested that Guilhem raise an army and capture the Sara-

The cloister at St Guilhem-le-Désert

cent lands of Orange, across the Rhône. This Guilhem did, and in addition, first widowed and then married the beautiful Lady of Orange, Queen Orable, whose name can hardly have been her fortune! Guilhem promptly had her re-named Gibourac, which scarcely trips lightly off the tongue either. Between them they founded the House of Orange which, through various connections, now rules in the Netherlands.

In later life, Guilhem, who was alway pious, turned to religion, and seeking a spot far from the pleasures of his Court, endowed a monastery on the Hérault, and when he died he was buried there. Later on he was canonised and his monastery at St Guilhem became a pilgrimage centre, a stop on the route to Compostella.

The Abbey Church is beautiful, and very well preserved, although when it fell into ruin in the last century, part of the Romanesque cloister was sold to the Metropolitan Museum of Art in New York. Moves are afoot to get the missing part returned and, as all the rest has been beautifully restored, one can only hope that this will happen.

Before his death, Charlemagne had given the young Knight a reliquary cross, which contained pieces of the True Cross, and this Guilhem left to his Abbey, where it remains to this day. Little replicas, made in biscuit, are available in the Abbey Church, where they are said to give good protection against lightning. After the 'orages' that had rolled around the mountains recently, I thought it best to take two! The jewelled reliquary cross is borne in procession through the village once a year on St Guilhem's feast day, the 3rd May. Above the village, on the side of the cliff, you will notice the ruins of a castle, once the abode of a Saracen giant. This evil fellow, called Don Juan, was defeated by Guilhem in single combat.

St Guilhem is a perfect little village with, apart from the Abbey, beautiful houses in yellow stone, and a shady square, with a gushing fountain and a great plane tree, spreading its branches against the sun. The village has one excellent hotel, the Taverne de l'Escuelle.

Today, apart from tourism and the beautiful Abbey which attracts many visitors, the village has many artists, in little studios around the square. If peace, quiet and beauty are really necessary for the artist, which is by no means certain, then they could hardly do better than follow in the footsteps of St Guilhem, the soldier Knight, who found, after all his adventures, a lasting home in these remote mountains.

6

The Hérault Littoral;
Séte to Cap d'Agde

From St Guilhem-le-Désert, we go south again, past La Clamouse, and through Gignac to the pleasant town of Clermont l'Hérault. Grapes grow as plentifully around Clermont as elsewhere in Hérault, but here they are table grapes, for the growing of which Clermont is the leading centre in France. Clermont is close to another natural wonder, the Cirque de Mourèze.

In the centre of the town is the Church of St Pierre, built in the late thirteenth century, and fortified during the Hundred Years War. It maintains a military air today, one of the weathervanes of the church being the figure of a mounted Knight with a couched lance. The church is lighter and more interesting than many French churches having suffered less in the Wars of Religion. It has some beautiful stained glass in a rose window, above the nave, and one or two interesting tombs and coffin lids, one of which, that of a soldier, is preserved inside the church, carved with bones, swords and teardrops. Outside the Cathedral a daily market takes place, and from here it is an easy walk uphill through the old streets of the town to the Château.

Leaving Clermont to head South, brings us to the medieval town of Pézenas, and by that step, to the seventeenth-century dramatist, Molière. Molière, whose real name was Jean-Francois Baptiste Poquelin, lived in Pézenas, lodging with his friend, the barber, Monsieur Gély. Here he wrote his first successful play, *Les Precieuses Ridicules*, which was later performed before Louis XIV at Vaux-le-Vicomte, on the fatal evening when Fouquet, who was Minister of Finance to Louis, and had been robbing the royal treasury for years, finally over-reached himself. Molière's play was the one bright spot in the King's evening and probably the only point at which he stopped grinding his teeth in fury, as the extent of Fouquet's peculations dawned on him. A few days later, Fouquet was in the Bastille, and Molière was the Court's favourite playwright. Pézenas has not

Pézenas

Sailing on the Bassin de Thau at Mèze

forgotten Molière, and there is a statue to him in the Place de 14 Juillet.

From the Square, the local Syndicate has had the excellent idea of signposting a walking tour through the old streets of the town. The town is full of fine old buildings, including the inevitable Commanderie, and old Pézenas is a town frozen in the eighteenth century. The old houses, narrow streets, balconies and shutters, are exactly as aged and lived in as they were then and, indeed, because of this, the town is frequently used as a location by film companies making historical pictures.

The Templar Commanderie, later owned by the Knights of St John, is in excellent condition while, in the back streets, are lots of little boutiques and workshops. The town was once the home of the Princes of Conti, who were Governors of Languedoc and patrons of Molière. For sheer style, Pézenas ought to be better known, and is a necessary stop in any tour of Languedoc.

From Pézenas we go across country through Montagnac to the lit-

The quay at Sète

tle port of Mèze, in the Bassin de Thau. Mèze lies on the north shore
of the Bassin, and devotes itself to some tourism, as a centre for
water sports, and to fishing, especially for oysters and mussels. The
palisades and fences of the oyster beds stretch far out into the Bassin,
and for miles along the north shore. It is through the Bassin that the
Canal du Midi finally reaches the sea at our next stop, the town of
Sète.

Sète, or Cette, as it used to be called, is my favourite stop on the
Languedoc littoral. Sète was built by the orders of Louis XIV's great
minister, Jean-Baptiste Colbert, to be the country's chief Mediterra-
nean port, and the terminus for the Canal du Midi. Construction
commenced in 1666, and three years later Paul Riquet, builder of the
Canal, was also charged with completing the wharfs and docks.
When the work was finally completed, Colbert came with a crowd of
Court dignitaries to open the Port, amid scenes of great rejoicing.
Two singular events marked the affair; the first being the creation, by
a local chef, of a special dish, the *Sole Colbert*, and the second was

The quay at Sète (another view)

The 'joute'

the presentation of water sports, including the now celebrated *joute* or water jousting, which dates back to the fourteenth century.

This is still the centrepiece of all festivities at Sète, and in other little ports along the coast. The jousters are now formed into clubs, which compete with each other on most weekends. The visitor stands a good chance of seeing the sport somewhere along the coast on most Sunday afternoons in summer, especially during August.

Two boats, one red and one blue, bearing flags and drummers or trumpeters, each rowed by eight oarsmen and carrying the jousters on a high platform, are rowed against each other. The jouster, who stands on an elevated platform some fifteen feet high, is armed with a short lance, ten feet in length, and protects himself with a wooden shield. A good thrust topples one or other headlong into the waters of the harbour, amid laughter, cheers and jeers from the crowd and fellow competitors. Each jouster must fell three opponents in each round, and the sport is quite skilful, taking years of practice to reach championship standard. It is all great fun and delights the onlooker today as much as it did in Colbert's time, three hundred years ago. Luckily, the jousters also enjoy their sport as well, and I noticed that the Sète team, when turning up recently to fight Agde, were accompanied by several lovely young ladies and twenty-five crates of beer! Over the last three centuries the sport has developed its own customs and traditions. In club jousts the married men are always in the blue boat and the bachelors in the red one. Also by tradition, it is the fishermen of the port who joust under blue colours.

Sète is built on or around the Mont St Clair, one of the two rocky outcrops on the coast, with wonderful views over the harbour and the Bassin de Thau. Sète is a major Mediterranean port, second only to Marseilles, and the chief wine port of France. It is also a big fishing port, the boats pulling into the fish dock in the heart of the town along the Quai de Bosc, where there is a whole row of excellent seafood restaurants. Here one can try *Sole Colbert*, the sole somewhat smaller than the one found in colder northern waters. If you feel like a snack, or want a centrepiece for a picnic, then try a *tielle,* a fish pie

Tielle and Seafood stalls at Sète

or pasty, a speciality of the town and really delicious. The first thing I do on arriving in Sète is to go down to the Quai de Bosc for a *tielle* and a glass of *Gris-de-Gris*. *Tielle* can be eaten cold or the stall-holders will heat them up for you. Either way they are a feast and a good introduction to the local food.

The cuisine of Languedoc Roussillon does not have the same elevated position in the French gastronomic league as does the cuisine of Normandy or Perigord. It is more noted for quantity than quality, as is, presumably, the case with the wine.

This said, the overall standard of cooking is as high as anywhere in France, and the area does possess, or at least contain, some fine dishes of its own.

Castelnaudary, between Carcassonne and Toulouse is reputedly the home of *Cassoulet*, a sort of bean and bacon stew, which can be found in all parts of France, but is especially excellent, and very filling, in the area of its home town. Sète, as we have noticed, is famous for sea food, especially sole and sardines, which are grilled over an open fire and eaten with the fingers. *Soupe de poisson,* and *soupe au pistou* are two other excellent local dishes. The local meat is excellent, sometimes obtained from bulls killed in the arena, and by some miracle the restaurants manage to serve it as you want it, a feat that seems to defeat British restaurants. If you want your steak *saignant* (rare); *à point,* (medium); or *bien cuit,* (well done), you have only to say which and your wish will be granted. Lamb or mutton from the Causses and *garrigue* is also excellent, while the streams and rivers provide trout and fresh-water crayfish.

Cheese is another strong point, in both senses of the word. Roquefort cheese is world famous, and for something lighter, *fromage de Chèvre,* from goats milk is very good. The great sauce of Languedoc is *aioli,* which is a rich garlic sauce, rather like tartare or mayonnaise, and this comes with a range of dishes, but especially with fish.

The range of fruit is particularly wide, and runs from olives and grapes, to apples, oranges, pears, lemons, peaches and nectarines. A typical meal would be *Soupe de Poisson,* a steak or *gigot* of lamb with *pommes de terre frites* and a salad, *fromage de Roquefort,* and a dish of fruit, accompanied by a bottle (or two) of *Gris-de-Gris*.

The local wines, especially the *Gris-de-Gris* rosés go particularly well with such a meal, and gastronomic expert or not, the traveller will find little to complain of in the restaurants of Languedoc-Roussillon.

Sète is the birthplace of the poet and writer Paul Valery, who was born in the town in 1871, and was buried there in 1945. He was a true *Sétois*, very fond of his native town and wrote his greatest work, the poem *Le Cimetière Marin*, about the cemetery by the sea there and, naturally enough, he was buried in the now famous cemetery. Valery was a member of the Academie Francaise, and a leader of the Symbolism School in literature. The town is proud of the connection and the people have built, below the Cimetière Marin, an open-air theatre, the Theatre de la Mer, where Valery's works are regularly heard. Sète is an agreeable town because it has both life and tradition. It is an interesting place to wander around, with ocean-going ships berthing at quays in the middle of the town, and a hearty bustle along the *quais* and by the fish port. The town is very popular with tourists, with over twelve miles of sandy beaches running from Sète towards Agde, and lots of good inexpensive hotels and restaurants. The Hotel Yalis, near the beach, is a hospitable family-run hotel, with a pool, a fine restaurant and a constant supply of cool drinks.

Tearing oneself away from Sète, one follows the road across the Causeway between the sea, the Bassin de Thau, towards Agde. All along the road, literally within a stone's throw of the sea, are large and well designed 'campings' full of colourful tents and caravans. In the summer months, camping along the coast can offer a most pleasant and inexpensive holiday. The 'campings' always advise the visitor to book, but being a wanderer, I never know where I will be on any particular evening, and have always found a spot to stay without much difficulty. 'Campings' are very large, and there are plenty of them, so if one is full, you simply move on to another. It is, though, a good idea to start looking at about five o'clock in the evening.

Agde is one of the oldest towns in Languedoc, founded by Greek seamen about 500 B.C., when it was called Agathee. Over-run by the Romans, the Visigoths and later by the Saracens, Adge continued as a trading port until the thirteenth century and was the principal centre in France for the Levant trade. It was regularly raided by the corsairs from the Barbary Coast, especially from Algiers, and it was against such raids that the Cathedral of St Etienne was gradually fortified. The Cathedral was built in the twelfth century and is constructed of volcanic stone from the nearby Mount St Loup, which gives it a rather worn, grey appearance, unusual in a country where most old buildings are constructed in warm yellow stone.

The Cathedral has one very curious feature, a hole in the roof,

The fortified Cathedral at Agde

through which the defenders of the place, up on the battlements, could obtain food and munitions, and from which the wounded could be lowered to shelter. The walls of the Cathedral are up to ten feet thick.

After the construction of Aigues-Mortes, and later Sète, Agde declined, and is now just a little, quite attractive, fishing port with an unusual small museum of local costume. Nowadays Agde is chiefly noted for traffic jams. All sorts of traffic seems to pour through the town, and delays in the centre of up to twenty minutes are quite normal.

On the coast nearby is the holiday resort of Le Grau d'Agde, reached along the banks of the Hérault, which flows into the sea here. Le Grau d'Agde is a typical little beach resort, with excellent bathing and very popular with *la jeunesse* who roar about the place on the inevitable scooters. A good spot to stay in Le Grau is at the local Logis de France, the El Rancho, right on the beach.

Not far away lies the new town and development of Cap d'Agde, a fashionable little resort and yachting centre, opened within the last few years and still in the course of construction. Cap d'Agde has 'taken off', as they say. Many of the new towns along the coast are still struggling to get going and attract sufficient people to make them viable economic propositions, but Cap d'Agde has passed this point, and is full of life. The marina, which can hold over a thousand boats, is full of craft, and the shops and cafés along the harbour have a nicely worn, lived-in look. Situated on the only headland between Sète and the Spanish frontier, the heights give the little resort some protection from the wind, which can be a problem on this coast. Just off the port lies the little island of Le Brescou, which was fortified by Vauban in the time of Louis XIV.

Near Cap d'Agde lies a naturist centre, a complex of shops, restaurants and apartments, designed especially for nudists. Along the South Coast are a growing number of beaches set aside for naturalists, and this healthy and attractive activity recruits an increasing number of followers every year, and, lest my reader suspects that life in a naturalist community is an endless round of basketball and avoiding cane chairs, I took my courage and towel in both hands and went to investigate.

All would-be naturalists should enroll in the *Federation Française de Naturisme,* which is based in the Rue St Denis in Paris and issues a little card, giving admission to the beaches. Usually there is a con-

The joust at Agde; the loser taking the plunge

trol at the entrance which may make a small charge, excludes voyeurs, and discourages cameras. Nudity is usually restricted, as much by convention as anything else, to the beach, and clothes are put on for meals, for shopping and in the evening. It is all extremely pleasant, and there can be no doubt that swimming and sunbathing is even more enjoyable unclad. It does seem wise to beware of excessive exposure to the sun, especially of those portions of one's anatomy which have not seen the light of day since birth. Otherwise, sitting down anywhere, let alone on a cane chair, may be a painful exercise for the next few days. The desire to get brown all over, or even here or there, is so much a part of the attraction of the Mediterranean, that I sometimes think statues should be erected by the grateful townspeople to two Englishmen who contributed considerably to this now fashionable pursuit. The first was the writer, Tobias Smollet, who was a great believer in sea bathing, not for his health but for sheer fun. The other was the English general of Victorian times, Lord de Ros, the first great advocate of sunbathing. Although an aristocrat, he would strip to the buff at the first peep of sunshine, and while doing so during the Crimean War got so badly sunburnt that he had to be invalided home.

The Languedoc-Roussillon littoral has over one hundred miles of perfect beaches, crowded every summer with thousands of sun and sea worshippers, not one of whom, I wager, knows about the early pioneers of this now universally accepted activity.

7

Béziers, The Minervois, Carcassonne

Some miles inland from Adge lies the town of Béziers, now a wine centre, and once an Albigensian stronghold. The town's great pride and claim to fame at present lies in its Rugby team, which provides most of the members of the French fifteen and enjoys international acclaim and widespread local support. Every other car seems to have an "*Allez Béziers*" sticker in the rear window, and the inhabitants, the Biterrois, have a cheeky, pugnacious, cheerful air.

In Languedocian terms the present Béziers is a new city, the old one, dating from Roman times, having been completely destroyed by the Albigensian Crusaders in 1209.

However pleasant Béziers is today, and it is indeed very pleasant, it also serves as the most potent reminder of the many appalling events in the Albigensian Crusade.

The teachers of history defend their interest, when necessary, by claiming that to study history is to see mankind in perspective, and historical persons and events objectively, in the round, complete in every detail. This may well be true, but if so, then it must also be admitted that the great lesson of history is that the human race are a pretty lousy lot!

The Albigensian Crusade, which we will discuss here, is a particularly nasty example of man's inhumanity to man. The king of France allowed his barons to ravage the South because, in the destruction of the Counts of Toulouse, he saw a way to extend his own domains. That this took place under cover of a Holy War, involving the death of tens of thousands of his fellow countrymen, bothered the King not at all.

Meanwhile, the Papacy and the priests of the Church, supported the Crusade and urged the Crusaders on, to the complete extirpation of the Cathars, because the pure life and the chaste conduct of the heretics showed up their own worldly behaviour in a bad light.

Typical of this approach was St Dominic. Returning through

Languedoc, Dominic attended a public dispute on religion, between a Cathar and a Catholic priest. Dominic, whatever his faults, knew honesty when he saw it, and was greatly impressed with the fervour and sincerity of the heritic although there can be no doubt that the Albigensian heresy was deeply offensive to the Church.

Dominic returned to Rome and, with the Pope's permission, founded his own order of preaching friars, the Dominicans, who took a leading role in the Albigensian Crusade, and thereafter went on to become the founding fathers of the Holy Office, the Inquisition. Why Dominic earned beatitude for this, only the saints could explain!

This chapter follows the main steps in the Crusade, the destruction of Béziers with which it opened, the fall of Carcassonne which broke the back, if not the heart, of the Cathar resistance, and leads us into the mountains of the Corbières, where the last Cathar Knights made their final gallant stand, at Montségur, and met a terrible end.

*　　　*　　　*

When the Crusaders came rampaging south, they skirted Carcas-

The Cathedral at Béziers

sonne, where the Courts of Toulouse were ready for them, and laid siege to Béziers, determined to frighten all the other heretic cities into surrender by making an example of the Cathars there. The *Biterrois*, then as now, were a pugnacious lot, and made a sortie against the camp of the Crusaders. Their attack was repulsed and the besiegers were able to enter the city on the heels of the fleeing Cathars. A terrible massacre then followed.

The soldiers, anxious not to kill true Christians within the walls, appealed to the Papal Legate for instruction on the execution of the heretics, only to be told, "Slay them all, God will know his own." Over twenty thousand of the population were killed and the town burned to the ground. It did not really recover until the last century, although in the meantime, in the seventeenth century, the city saw the birth of its favourite son, Paul Riquet, the architect of the Canal du Midi. Riquet was born there in 1604, and a large statue in the Allées Paul Riquet, commemorates his name to this day. The Allées are the main promenade of the town, and contain a daily market of flowers, fruit, wine, or some type of agricultural activity. Below the Allées lie the gardens of the Plateau des Poetes, full of flowers, with ponds and ducks, a pleasant spot for a doze on a hot afternoon.

Porch carving, the Cathedral, Béziers

The Cathedral of St Nazaire, which towers over the River Orb, was rebuilt after the massacre, and records some of the terrible events of those days in carvings over the door to the nave. In the cloisters, a nice touch is a tablet commemorating the troubadours of Languedoc, who, in the twelfth century contributed so much to the growth of civilization in the feudal world of Western Europe. Georges Duhamel wrote that wine is a symbol of civilization, and what wine lover could argue with that? Béziers' present prosperity is built on wine and the town has a wine museum in the old Dominican Church, where one can inspect the history of wine from Roman times to the present day, including the reconstruction of an old Béziers *auberge*, the Auberge du Coche d'Eau, which formerly housed passengers from the Canal du Midi. On 15th August each year, the Allées are the centre of the town's great *Feria*, or fair, with sport and bullfights, while a fountain near Riquet's statue flows with wine all day.

Visitors should not leave Béziers without going out on the Valras road and turning off to visit the spectacular series of locks, the Neuf Écluses, on the Canal du Midi, which runs through the outskirts of the town. A visit to the Neuf Écluses is a popular Sunday outing for the *Biterrois*. This was one of Paul Riquet's most ingenious locks, with nine chambers in series, running up like a staircase. When the upper pounds are cleared a great roaring wall of white water pours down through the sluices and the chambers below fill up with great rapidity, dropping the pleasure-boat and canal craft down rapidly to the levels below.

*   *   *

Valras-Plage, on the coast, about eight miles from Béziers, is the nearest seaside resort, and with a wide beach and some good little restaurants is the principal weekend retreat for the local people. Valras has taken to the bicycle and developed it into a major source of transport. Tandems, for up to five people, trishaws for up to ten people, and little side-by-side tricycles, circle the streets of the town, the riders yelling cheerfully at the pedestrians and at each other. To take a family cycle ride, with the whole family, including grandparents, on the same machine, is a popular evening excursion, and a side trip for

The Neuf Ecluces at Béziers

a bathe at Valras, makes a short break before we head off, through the Minevois, towards Carcassonne.

Leaving Béziers, our route lies North and West, towards Carcassonne, through the Minervois, and the first stop should be made at the old Gaulish Oppidum, or hill fort, at Ensérune, just south of the road to Capestang. You can spot the Oppidum from a long way away, perched high up on a hill which offers excellent views over the surrounding countryside.

Below the hills to the North lies the flat, curious, plain, once a lake, but laid out like a dartboard, with triangular fields seamed with irrigation channels all leading into a central boss. This curious plain dates back to pre-Gaulish times and acquired the present configuration from the layout of the irrigation system. The central ring marks the site of the original lake.

The Oppidum itself is largely Gaulish, and before the Romans came was one of the largest in Southern Gaul. The site was abandoned in the first century A.D. and present-day excavations are revealing many of the features of a Gallic Oppidum in its prime. A museum on the hill contains some fine exhibits.

North of Ensérune, on the road between Béziers and Carcassonne, lies the region known as the Minervois. This is a region devoted entirely to the cultivation of vines, and produces excellent red wines of VDQS standard. The Minervois is a small area, about ten miles wide and thirty miles long, penned between the Montagne Noire and the Central pass which divides the Pyrénées from the Massif Central.

The Minervois is full of delightful little towns, and a good centre for visiting the region is the Hotel-Chateau de Violet at Peyriac-Minervois, near Rieux.

Minervois wines, the production of which is the region's only industry, are the best reds in Languedoc. Most of them are of VDQS quality, and I understand from those who profess to know, that they improve with keeping.

North of the Minervois lie the dark peaks of the Montagne Noire. This is a wild range of hills on the southern limits of the Massif Central, and although crossed by a few roads, to Albi, or Castres, it remains a remote area, full of ravines and water courses.

The Montagne Noire was vital to Riquet when he planned the building of the Canal du Midi. His main problem was to ensure an adequate supply of water during the dry Mediterranean summer. Knowing that for at least four months of the year, his main sources,

The Gallic 'Oppidum' at Ensérune

on the Rivers Aude, Orb and Hérault, could dry up, he therefore tapped the rivers of the Montagne Noire, the Lampy, the Alzau and the Vernassore, and every stream of any size, and by a system of canals fed them into his vast dam at St. Férreol, above Castelnaudry.

Mazamet is the chief town of the Montagne Noire, on the road to Castres, and from here one can make a grand tour of this remote and interesting region. The traveller should make a point of heading west, above the Minervois, by remote roads, to Roquebrun, in the Valley of the Orb. Roquebrun, a recently created area of outstanding beauty, has a very mild climate, grows citrus fruits and is the gateway to the Espinouse, and Languedoc's northern frontier, the heights of the *Parc Naturel du Haut Languedoc. The Parc Naturel du Haut Languedoc* lies on the northern border of the province, and is remarkable, even in an area of natural splendour such as this. As you will have gathered I have a taste for the high, lonely places and, if you share it, the Espinouse and the Montagne Noire are not to be missed.

Back on the main road which runs through the pass between Narbonne and Toulouse, we can visit Lézignan, a major wine town of the Corbières, before proceeding to one of the major tourist attractions of France, the Cité of Carcassonne.

Coming from Toulouse, the spectacle of the Cité, perched on its hill, in the afternoon sunlight, is a magnificent sight, and for me at least, not a whit marred by the knowledge that the Cité is a nineteenth-century reconstruction, and not the original town. As with so many ancient towns and buildings, the stone of Carcassonne was carried away by later builders, until the once great Cité was a ruin.

A number of guides write in a somewhat carping high-toned manner about the activities of the nineteenth-century architect and restorer, Eugene Viollet-le-Duc, who, finding Carcassonne an abandoned place, due for demolition, suggested to the French Government of the day that it could, and should, be restored as a perfect example of fourteenth- and fifteenth-century French military architecture. Viollet-le-Duc undertook the work; he had already restored the Cluniac Abbey at Vézelay, and his work there has since met with the approval of no less an authority than Lord Clark, which is good enough for me.

Viollet-le-Duc felt that, as an example of medieval military architecture, Carcassonne was unrivalled, and his restoration, which employed as much of the old Cité remains as possible, plus careful research for the reconstruction of those parts that had vanished, has resulted in the Cité as we see it today, and to my mind he made a splendid job of it. Carcassonne does not have the stark soldierly air of Aigues-Mortes, and is altogether more romantic, but here, one feels, the troubadours would have felt completely at home.

The Cité is encircled by two rings of walls, between which lie the *Lices*, or lists. Here the tournaments took place, and the garrison paraded for drill and skill at arms contests. The visitor enters between the *Lices*, through the Porte Narbonnaise, and up narrow medieval streets to the central keep. From here, conducted tours, lasting about an hour, can take you on a circuit of the ramparts, and tell something of the Cité's history.

Carcassonne, on the River Aude, was the capital of the Viscounty of the same name, a cadet of the House of Toulouse. The Viscounty knew prosperity for many years until in 1209 the then Viscount, Raymond-Roger Trencavel closed his gates against the Albigensian Crusaders of Simon de Montfort, to protect his subjects, who were, in the main, Cathar supporters.

Following the massacre at Béziers, the Crusaders sat down before Carcassonne, and while treating with the enemy, Raymond-Roger was seized and later murdered. Carcassonne fell and became a Royal City, and the fortifications were later improved by such noted figures as Alphonse of Poitiers, the brother of St Louis, and Philip the Bold. So splendid were they that when the Black Prince came down on Languedoc in 1355, he took one look at the walls and led his army away, although he burnt the lower town before doing so.

As we have said elsewhere, during the Middle Ages, the Pyrénées divided nothing, and the frontier of the Spanish Kingdom of Aragon lay well inside what is now France.

Carcassonne lies in the middle of the great pass that leads up to Toulouse, and therefore holds the southern gateway to the heart of France, but could never have survived as a frontier town in the age of artillery. She was protected by a string of castles called, collectively, the "Sons of Carcassonne", but when in 1659, France over-ran Roussillon, the frontier moved back to the Pyrénées and the main frontier town became Perpignan. Carcassonne went into a decline from which it took Viollet-le-Duc to awaken it.

Today, although the work of preservation still continues, Carcassonne is a wonderful place to visit, and must be one of the most photographed towns in France. The whizzing and clicking on the walls would be music to the ears of Mr Agfa or Mr Kodak. There is a

The 'Lices' at Carcassonne

The Keep in Carcassonne

narrow footpath round the outside of the walls, from which you can obtain magnificent views to the Cévennes, and the far Pyrénées.

Carcassonne supplements her attractions by holding each July a major Arts Festival, with plays, orchestral concerts and poetry readings.

All this succeeds in attracting visitors to the Cité and it is sad to say that they get less than a warm welcome when they arrive. The waiters, shopkeepers and bank cashiers of the Cité seem to be drawn from three sorts of people, those who are grasping, those who are surly, and those who are both! Luckily in the Ville Basse, below the walls of the Cité, the natives are less hostile.

South of Caracassonne, through Limoux, one can head south and west and travel across wild country, out of Languedoc into Ariège, through Lavelanet, to the Castle of Montségur, where the last of the Cathar Knights were finally overwhelmed. The Albigensian Crusade began in 1208. It was not until 1243 that the last embers were gathered into Montségur.

Montségur was, if the remaining ruins are anything to go by, a mighty castle. Here the Cathars obtained aid and supplies from nearby Aragon, and mounted raids against their persecutors in the North. In 1243 the French garrison from Carcassonne marched against Montségur, and laid seige to it for nine months.

Eventually the garrison was starved out and forced to surrender, and the final scenes were as typically cold-blooded as the rest of the Crusade had been. As the gates were opened, some of the besiegers moved in among the Cathars, taking their weapons and stripping the armour from their emaciated bodies. Many more turned away from the walls, hunting through the camp and then scattering over the countryside in a locust-horde, all seeking the necessary ingredient to end the Crusade — firewood.

On the morning after the Castle fell, the garrison were led out to the rocky plain below the walls, and there, two hundred of them, the last of the Cathars, were burned alive. The place is still called the Field of Burning.

*   *   *

West of Carcassonne it is about twenty miles up the Pass to the town of Castelnaudary, home of *Cassoulet*, and major port on the Canal du Midi. Most French towns of any antiquity announce their attractions to the visitor with ornate signboards on the approach roads; *"Son Château XIV"; "Sa Eglise Romanesque"*; and so on. Castelnaudary does likewise, with signs in praise of *Son Cassoulet*, her stew! Castelnaudary is the home of *Cassoulet*, a thick, warming dish, containing mutton, bacon, garlic, beans and onions, and while you can obtain it all over Languedoc — indeed, all over France — it is the speciality of Castelnaudary, and the best place to try it for the first time.

In the Grand Bassin of Castelnaudary, the Blue Line fleet of pleasure cruisers is based, and from here one can tour the Canal du Midi, and via that link, cruise over four hundred miles of canals in the Midi. This seems a good point at which to discuss at greater length the Canal du Midi, and its architect, Paul Riquet.

The Canal du Midi, which forms part of a waterway connecting the Atlantic with the Mediterranean, begins at Toulouse, runs across Languedoc and, via the Bassin du Thau, reaches the Mediterranean at Sète. It has a total length of one hundred and fifty miles, and after construction was completed in 1681 it was regarded as the engineering wonder of Western Europe. It remains a splendid piece of work, and for both beauty and utility is unsurpassed among the world's canals.

Paul Riquet, son of a prosperous lawyer, was born in Béziers in June 1604. He was a passionate Occitain, refusing to speak French, and became a collector of the salt tax in Languedoc, an office of profit under the French Crown.

He was fifty before he began planning the Canal, although the project had interested him since childhood. In 1662 he laid out his ideas in a letter to Colbert, chief minister to Louis XIV, and after the inspection and approval of a Royal Commission, Riquet received the go-ahead in 1666.

As has been mentioned earlier, the nub of Riquet's plan was the means to ensure an adequate supply of water all year round, by tapping all available local rivers, building dams, and thereby, with feeder channels, see that his Canal never ran dry, however dry the summer might be.

If this could be assured then the advantages and profits were enormous. Riquet himself stated the case clearly, in his letter to Colbert. A Canal, he wrote, would avoid the passage round the Straits of Gibraltar, thus diminishing the revenues of the King of Spain. It would reduce the risk of attack from the Barbary Corsairs. It would also give a short link between the two seas, and the tolls charged on the shipping would make a fortune for the Crown and the Canal proprietors.

From this declaration two points emerge. Firstly, that the Canal was designed to accommodate the sea-going coastal vessels of the

Statue of Riquet, Béziers

A cruiser on the Canal du Midi

day, and secondly that it was to be a joint venture of the French Crown and private enterprise.

The Canal was to be six feet deep and over fifty feet wide, supplied with locks, tunnels and passing places, and twelve thousand men laboured for fourteen years until the work was completed.

The task would have daunted lesser men, and Riquet ran into all manner of opposition. He had to levy taxes in Languedoc to pay for the work, and his tax collectors met with stiff resistance from the local people. Even the obvious advantages that the Canal would bring were no encouragement to the people who had to pay for it.

Riquet was a lawyer, not an engineer, and although he had able assistants, such a vast engineering project had never been undertaken before, and the problems that arose had to be overcome by trial and error, and they occurred.

One of Riquet's greatest feats was the construction of the dam at St Ferréol. This is a mammoth affair over one hundred feet high and

Traffic on the Canal du Midi

four hundred and fifty feet thick at the base. It dams the River Laudot, and at the foot the pressure sprays out a jet of water rising fifty feet into the air; a most attractive touch.

Indeed, the pleasantest thing about the Canal du Midi for the layman, with only a slight interest in the technical details of canals, is that it is so attractive. One can spot the route of the Canal from miles away, by the lines of shady plane trees which line the banks and, following the contours of the land as it does, it follows a weaving, winding course which is very pleasing to the eye.

Plane trees were planted all along the route as it was found that their roots bound the earth banks tightly, and gave protection against erosion. The locks are clever affairs, and the whole route from Castelnaudary to Sète is across some of the most delightful country in Languedoc.

The best and most pleasant way to see the Canal du Midi, is to tour it by boat. Many people bring their own boats down the French canal system to do so, but in recent years an English company has established itself in the Grand Bassin at Castelnaudary, and with a fleet of over fifty cruisers, offers holidays all over the Southern canal system, including the non-tidal lengths of the Canal du Midi.

Riquet's financial support from Colbert ran out in 1677, and Riquet had to finance the rest of the Canal out of his own pocket. Undaunted, although he was by now over seventy, Riquet did so, and the Canal was duly completed in 1681, although Riquet, alas, didn't live to see it.

In 1680, knowing he was dying, Riquet sent for his son, Jean, who was by then in charge of the works.

"Where is my Canal?" he asked.

"Just one league to go" replied Jean.

"One league" murmured Riquet, and died.

Few men can become legends in their own lifetime or create things that remain in use long after their death. Riquet did both these things and his Canal du Midi is as beautiful and successful today, three hundred years after his death, as it was on the day it opened.

8

Narbonne, The Corbières, Rennes-Le-Chateau

I don't like large towns, but I like Narbonne. Perhaps it is the sight, from far off, of the great Cathedral and fortress rearing up over the roofs, or perhaps it is that after a long trip it is nice to relax in one of the cafés by the Canal de la Robine. Whatever the reason, Narbonne, for me anyway, has charm.

It is an old city, once the capital of Southern Gaul, and later under the Romans, the centre of the *Colonie Narbonensis,* and a major seaport.

Later, in the fifth century, the Visigoths arrived and, wise folk, adopted Narbonne as their capital. Then followed the usual series of invasions, especially by the Saracens.

The Merovingian King, Pepin the Short, captured Narbonne in 759 A.D. Charlemange created a dukedom out of the old Roman province, and it prospered for many years before the harbour silted up and the ships moved away. The powerful Bishops of Narbonne controlled the Dukedom in medieval times, and it was one of them, after being raised to the Papacy as Clement IV, who began the construction of the Cathedral in 1272. The Cathedral today is a huge place, hung with tapestries and containing magnificent vaulting. This Cathedral is less stark than most French churches, although as usual, most of the tombs have been defaced. Off the Passage de l' Ancre, a part of the cloister has been made into a little museum of medieval sculpture, all in excellent condition, and most interesting. This is reached by passing the Hotel de Ville, which looks like a grim medieval fortress, but was actually built by Viollet-le-Duc in the last century. It had me fooled until I enquired, and mock Gothic or not, goes very well against the background of the old Cathedral.

Behind the Hotel de Ville lies the old fortified Palace of the Archbishops, dating from the early twelfth century, with later additions. The New Palace, which was added in the fourteenth century, houses the Museum of Art and Ceramics, and is reached up a long, leg-test-

112

ing staircase. As I staggered to the top, stairs not being my forté, the attendant told me that in the seventeenth century the Bishops used to ride up on little mules, an excellent old custom which should have been retained.

The museum has some excellent collections of alabaster, and Limoges ceramics, and a wide and tasteful collection of paintings. The Prehistory Museum, which is also in the Palace, is full of Gallic and Neolithic tools and artifacts, all discovered in the region around Narbonne.

*　　*　　*

In 1642, Narbonne was Richelieu's base for the siege of Perpignan, the final step in fulfillment of his three lifelong ambitions; to humble the Huguenots, crush the nobles, and give France secure frontiers. All these steps, as we have seen, have left evidence in Languedoc in the shape of the ruined castles of the old nobility, for Richelieu decreed that all but frontier castles must be dismantled, while on the desolate Causse, and Cévennes, the last of the Huguenots still lingers. Here, on the doorstep of Roussillon, at the end of his life, he saw his last ambition about to be realized.

However, as had happened so often during his life, Richelieu was forced to campaign with only one eye watching the enemy, and the other looking behind him, for yet again there was a plot against his life.

The war with Spain had been going on for seven years, and even if the cause for starting the conflict, the detention of the Bishop of Trier, was thought to be petty, the aim was far from trivial. This was to drive the Spanish beyond the Pyrénées, and if Perpignan fell, with the Catalans already in revolt, then Richelieu's life's work would be complete. However, at this moment, the current favourite of Louis XIII, Henri d'Effiat, Maquis de Cinq-Mars, was plotting against Richelieu's life.

Seventeenth-century monarchs must have been a strange lot. James I and Charles I of England, both made fools of themselves over their favourites, and Louis XIII was a complete idiot over Cinq-Mars. They can hardly have all been homosexual, and even if they seem to have viewed women as rather tiresome creatures, many red-blooded men have done the same, with no real harm done.

113

Louis XIII elevated Cinq-Mars to a position of great influence, making him the Master of Horse, and he was generally known as Monsieur Le Grand. All this at seventeen, and not surprisingly, it went to Cinq-Mars' head and led to him losing it!

Cinq-Mars was persuaded that if he could dispose of Richelieu, he could rule the King, and France, and in this he made his fatal error, for he plotted to betray the French army besieging Perpignan, to the Spanish. In this he misjudged both the Cardinal and the King, for he should have known that the Cardinal's spies would discover his plot and that the King would show him no mercy over it. Louis was first and last a King; in between he might have wavered somewhat, but he never forgot his duty in the end.

Cinq-Mars was arrested in a house by the Church of St Paul in Narbonne, the *Maison des Trois Nourrices*, or the 'House of the Three Wet Nurses', so called, I imagine, from the figures of the very ample and well-endowed caryatids supporting the main window, although there are in fact five of them. Cinq-Mars may have been very handsome, but he cannot have been very bright. The *'Trois Nourrices'* is hardly the least conspicuous house in the city.

On 12th October, Richelieu was able to write, "Perpignan is in our

The 'Maison des Trois Nourrices', Narbonne

hands and Monsieur Le Grand is in the other world.! His mission was complete. The Spanish, of course, fought on, but with the fall of Perpignan the end was never in doubt, and in 1659 all Catalonia, east of the Pyrénées, was ceded to France.

The Church of St Paul, near the *Trois Nourrices,* is a gloomy place, only remarkable for the holy water stoup near the door which contains the carving of a frog. Legend has it that, long ago, a frog hopped into the stoup and joined the choir in singing. For this temerity it was turned into stone, and so far, no maiden has ventured to see if a kiss would transform it into a handsome prince!

*   *   *

Leaving Narbonne, the road runs south and then west for a tour of the Corbières, those green vine-clad hills which dominate the coastal littoral below Narbonne.

In the Corbières lies the Abbey of Fontfroide, now a private home, but beautifully restored and open to guided tours. It was a Cistercian Abbey and dates from the twelfth century. From here, the signposted *Route des Corbières* takes the traveller on a trip across the hills, past two ruined castles, those of Durfort and Termes. These were part of the defensive ring of castles built around Carcassonne, known collectively as the 'Sons of Carcassonne'. It is interesting to plot the sites of these medieval castles on a map for the concentration is all well north of the Pyrénées, a visual reminder, yet again, that for most of French history, indeed until the mid-seventeenth century, the Spanish frontier lay well inside the borders of modern France.

This *Route,* the *D212,* is very narrow and winding and it takes a long time to reach St Paul de Fenouillet, and turn west again for Quillan. The hills south of St Paul are the Fenouilledes, which produce a nice dry wine.

Further down the valley, Muscat is grown, while in the Corbières, the growth is mostly for reds. The Corbières produce some very pleasant wine, much of it, like that of the Minervois, of VDQS standard. It is always a good idea in the Midi, to drink the local wine where it exists, and Corbières wines are very good and improve with keeping. The area also produces a great party wine, the Blanquette de Limoux, a light, sparkling wine, which comes to suit all tastes, from sweet to dry.

115

Forking left at Caudies, one road for Quillan climbs up through the Fôret de Fanges, and round the corkscrew turns of the Col St Louis, which is just like a spiral staircase. The Fôret is a great place for wild life, and as the car passed, an eagle soared out of the trees to swoop across the bonnet of the car and climb off to the Corbières, with great beats of his powerful wings.

The main road to Quillan, the 117, is an equally exciting route, running through gorges and tunnels in the rock, with the river foaming below. At Quillan, the River Aude reappears, running under the bridges of the town and along the walls of the riverside houses, and the route turns north here, to Couiza where one can visit the fine castle of the Ducs de Joyeuse, before turning left for a trip up the mountain to the mysterious hilltop village of Rennes-le-Château.

*   *   *

The strange history of Rennes-le-Château is well known in the Midi, if not totally understood, and the story is a modern mystery of quite disturbing proportions. Until the end of the last century, Rennes was a typical village, rather smaller and more beautiful than most, but with no other claim to fame. Then, in the 1880s, the village church acquired a new *Curé*, Berengar Saunière, who at first seemed a perfectly normal village priest, going about his pastoral duties, such as they were, in a satisfactory manner.

Then, quite suddenly, Saunière acquired great wealth. A huge fortune, out of nowhere, came to be at his disposal. How Saunière got his money he refused to say — or rather, he offered various incorrect explanations, but the fact that he had a fortune was, and is, undisputed. One generally accepted estimate is that in ten years he spent over a million pounds, when his income in the same period was not above a few thousand.

He built the village a water tower, improved the road from Couiza, bought himself a house, redecorated the little church, and spent lavishly. Before long, lacking an explanation, legends and strange tales began to circulate. It was, and is, said that Saunière had found the secret treasure of the Visigoths. Others said his money was a hoard of the Cathars, and others that it was the lost treasure of the Knights Templar. Saunière claimed, blandly, that he merely sold

The graveyard at Rennes-le-Château

masses for the sick, and received gifts or donations in response to the advertisements for aid which he placed in religious papers.

No such advertisements have been found, and no heavy post reached the village, and from their own experience his colleagues and superiors in the Church must have known this explanation was false. In his accounts, Saunière had to pad his bills, to account for his expenditure, and from the story thus far, two mysteries still remain. Where did Saunière get his money? It certainly was not from selling masses for the sick, and no church in France received anything like the money from donations that Sauniere would have had to receive to spend as he did. Secondly, given that he had wealth, what did he do with it? Why all the secrecy, and why did he die apparently penniless? His housekeeper, who was with him all these years, must have known something, yet she too died a pauper, shortly after Saunière. She, surely, must have known his secret.

Now, it might seem that all this is smoke without fire. A man is perfectly entitled to inherit, earn, or otherwise acquire, wealth, without having to account for it to anyone except the Income Tax Man. Hidden treasure is, of course, always fascinating and for that reason alone, Rennes would be interesting, but what really makes the place fascinating is the air of menace that hangs over the whole story.

Local historians, who are better placed than most to dig into the background of Saunière's strange life, are at dagger-thrusts with each other over their findings and conclusions and the only point of agreement seems to be an underlying conviction that the story of Rennes has still some surprises in store.

All this, of course, arouses speculation that the source of Saunière's treasure is still in Rennes-le-Château and, increasingly, people come in search of it. Meanwhile, historians, local, national and international, dispute the source and disposal of his wealth in the strongest terms. The most popular theory is that he chanced on a treasure of the Knights Templar. That, at least, is the firm conviction of the villagers, and it is possible. The Order of the Temple was incredibly rich. The Order's income in the thirteenth century exceeded six million pounds a year, a sum impossible to calculate today. When the Order was suppressed, many Knights fled south to Spain, sheltering for the night perhaps at the Templar castle of Blanchefort, just below Rennes. If the Templars there had a treasure, they couldn't flee across the Pyrénées loaded with sacks of silver pennies, and they certainly wouldn't leave it behind for Philip the Fair's officers. Perhaps they decided to hide it in the church at Rennes. Who knows?

This brings us to the church itself, and here the mystery not only deepens but becomes disturbing and unpleasant. The church at Rennes gives even insensitive travellers a touch of the horrors! It dates from the Romanesque period and was completely redecorated by Sauniére in the early years of this century. It was done with much money and appalling taste. The church is kept locked, but the key can be obtained from the little shop by the door and, once inside, the decor strikes the visitor like a blow. The church is garish, spangled, and washed in blue and rose. Just inside the door, bearing the holy water stoup on his shoulders, is the life-size figure of a crouching demon, picked out in evil colours, with the finger and toe nails obscenely long. Who would place the Devil's statue in a church? The stations of the cross also seem odd, with skulls as a frequent motif, while on the wall facing the altar is a large relief of the Sermon on the Mount. On it, behind the listening crowd, on the ground and ignored by all, is a large bag of money. It is very obviously there for a reason, and what can the reason be?

The cross at Rennes carries not Christ crucified, but the Virgin! Some people maintain that the church is full of clues to the source of Saunière's treasure. Others hint that he was a sorcerer or involved in some form of Black Magic. The church could easily convince one of that; Saunière, for all his obscurity, knew people who were involved in the occult, and kept in regular contact with them.

Rennes is a beautiful place, and it is quite a relief to get out of the church, whatever its message, and up onto the windy hill above.

The views are splendid, but the spirit of Saunière lingers on even here, although he died in 1917. So many questions remain unanswered. Why did his Bishop not insist on an explanation? If Saunière found and sold a vast quantity of fourteenth-century coins, would not the disposal have been noticed by coin collectors? Why did he cultivate the friendship of people interested in the occult? Why have all Saunière's records disappeared from the archives? Why was the local bishop so reticent about his most interesting subordinate? There is also the theory that the money is the embezzled fortune of Nicolas Fouquet, Louis XIV's minister, and that the clues are contained in a painting he commissioned from Poussain. Why all the secrecy; all the evasion? Why the hint of danger?

The sinister mystery of Rennes-le-Château grows almost yearly. At the end of the last war, three bodies were discovered buried in the

The church porch at Rennes-le-Château

village, and these are still unidentified, while, as late as 1973, the owner of Saunière's house in Rennes was ambushed and his car machine-gunned. It all provides the ingredients for a mystery in which Sherlock Holmes would have delighted. But not me! I am not very interested in the Templars' treasure, or in whatever was the source of Saunière's wealth, but Sauniere himself is a different matter. There is something very odd about a priest who would decorate his own church in such a fashion and put outside, on the lintel, as a finishing touch, the words:

Terribilis est locus Iste

which translated means:

This Place is Terrible

*   *   *

For all its wild, windswept charm, Rennes gives me a strong touch of the Gothic horrors, and it was no hardship to return down the moun-

The Lydia Casino, Barcarès, Roussillon

tain and head back to the coast, to the little resort of Port-Leucate.

On the Languedoc-Roussillon coast lies a whole series of new towns, the outposts of our promised future style of life. We have already visited Le Grande Motte and Cap d'Agde. On the Languedoc littoral, south-east of Narbonne, lies a further group of new coastal resorts, all recently constructed and, like La Grande Motte, backed by wide shallow lagoons or *étangs*. Coming down the coast from the North, these resorts are at Gruissan, Port-Leucate, and just across the border into Roussillon, Port-Barcarès. One can see one reason for the development of these resorts when caught in the vast volume of traffic streaming past them on the road to Spain. Languedoc-Roussillon has as much to offer as the Spanish resorts, with better food and smaller crowds.

Leucate lies on the natural causeway which separates the huge, shallow, Étang de Leucate from the open sea, and is a growing resort, well supplied with shops, cinemas, bars, restaurants and a great stretch of wide, sandy beach. The *étang* behind Leucate is a sailing area, though only deep enough for dinghies, while Leucate itself

121

The stranded Lydia at Barcarès

is a great yachting centre with an expanding marina able to handle over a thousand boats, and a sailing school. Nearby is another naturist beach, and the whole area, if a little plagued by strong winds, is a perfect summer resort.

The Étang de Leucate is a strange sight at weekends, for people swarm out of the nearby towns to fish in the shallow waters, and stand half a mile from shore, still only ankle deep, searching on the bed of the *étang* for oysters or mussels.

Other, bolder spirits, plunge into the deeper areas in wet suits, while from the shore, their relatives watch anxiously and get a fire going to cook the forthcoming catch. On the beaches, incidentally, the *gendarmerie* run life-saving posts, indicating the degree of risk at sea by a series of flags. When the red flag is flying bathing is prohibited, although it should be stated that on the hundred and forty miles of beach between the Rhône and the Pyrénées, the bathing generally is very safe.

Leucate seems to be the family resort, with the local night life concentrated more at Le Barcarès, a short mile down the beach. Each new resort has tried to think up a style of architecture different from the rest, and Barcarès has an attractive series of buildings and, as an added attraction, high and dry on the sand, the large steamship *Lydia*. This former merchant ship has been converted into an amusement centre, with restaurants, bars and a large discotheque, much frequented by the local *jeunesse dorée*. Those who enjoy a good meal in quieter surroundings should visit the Auberge de la Pin in nearby St Laurant de La Salanque.

The new developments will be watched with interest everywhere, for, if it is true as we are continually being told, that we are moving into an age of leisure, then such vacation centres will become the footholds for a new age.

The curious thing about leisure today is that is seems to demand constant activity. Each of the new French resorts offers a wide range of pastimes, as if modern man is incapable of ever sitting still. These resorts have few hotels, as yet, and it is usually necessary to rent an apartment from an owner, if you wish to stay there.

This flat, sandy coast, which stretches for almost a hundred and fifty miles from the Rhône to the Pyrénées must inevitably become one of Europe's great summer playgrounds. One hopes it will not disappear under an avalanche of hoardings and bill-boards, and that the great wild places and sea-scapes of the present time are retained. So far, at least, there is reason to believe that they will be.

9

Roussillon, Perpignan, The Cerdagne, Villefranche

On the coast road just below Port-Leucate, and before Barcarès, you cross out of Languedoc into Roussillon, the old French Catalonia, or the present-day *Département* of Pyrénées-Orientales, and once a great fief of the Kingdom of Aragon. Roussillon belonged to Aragon until it was gathered into a united Spain by Ferdinand in 1512. It passed into French hands under the Treaty of the Pyrénées in 1659. The first noticeable sign is that the flags change. Instead of red with the gold cross of Languedoc, you see the red and gold stripes of Roussillon, a former possession of Spain, and still in Spanish colours. Roussillon, much smaller than Languedoc, has much to recommend it, for it is truly a land of many seasons and enjoys an excellent climate, fine food and wine, and a great variety of scenery. The valleys of the Têt and Tech, the two great rivers of Roussillon, enjoy particularly mild weather, with many of the small towns along their course and in the nearby Aspres range of hills, being health resorts where mimosa blooms in February, and the orange blossom is out in March.

Before Perpignan, the capital of Roussillon, on the right of the road, lies the great fortress of Salses, built by the Spanish at the end of the fifteenth century, and later altered by Vauban. It is a transitional castle, and one of the few which bridge the gap between the days of the catapult and the days of cannon. From the road Salses does not appear very large, but as you approach you realise that it is built below ground level, like a bunker, and that the corner bastions have lost their tops. Vauban flattened them to make gun platforms and build the convex ramparts which would deflect a cannon ball, very much as present-day tank armour is sloped to deflect a shell. It is a beautiful place, well preserved and constructed of rosy brick and mellow stone, and no student of military fortification should miss a visit to this squat, solid fortress. Curiously enough Vauban's efforts were never put to the test. The castle had been besieged many times

The walls of Salses

The ramparts at Salses, Roussillon

before it finally fell to the French in 1642, but since then its role has been quite peaceful.

Salses produces a very palatable wine which can be bought at the co-operative in the village, and is the gateway to the wines of Rivesaltes, which are sold widely in the Midi, as an aperitif. Rivesaltes is also the birthplace of Marshal Joffre, Commander in Chief of the French armies in the first years of the Great War.

* * *

Perpignan, chief city of Roussillon, lies on the River Têt and looks like a capital. Indeed, for almost a century it was the capital of the briefly-lived Kingdom of Majorca.

James 1 of Aragon was a crusading monarch, who drove the Moslems from the Balearic Islands. On his death in 1278 he gave his principal domains, Aragon and the County of Barcelona, to his eldest son, Pedro III, and Majorca, Roussillon and his fief of the

French town of Montpellier to his second son, Jaime. This scattered collection became the Kingdom of Majorca, and three Kings ruled it from Perpignan, before the Aragonese decided to reclaim it in 1344. The last King of Majorca fled to France, and fought in the French army against the English at Crecy in 1346.

During this period, the great castle-palace of the Kings of Majorca was built, which is now better described as a citadel, having been developed by Vauban, and it still covers a large area above the town. Built of brick, interlaced here and there with linings of large stones from the local river beds, it was a formidable fortress, and is now used mainly for folklore exhibitions and dancing displays. The old walls, of which the Palace was the bastion, were later demolished, and as is quite customary, their position is now marked by boulevards. This is a useful relic of the old fortifications in many French towns, for naturally enough the walls circled the town and, once pulled down, made a perfect ring-road, to the relief of traffic planners in a later age. If you get a street map of an old French town, the present 'Toute Direction' road often follows the course of the old walls.

In the centre of the town stands the fortress of Le Castillet, a machiolated tower of brick, built in 1368 to form a bastion in the walls, and used later as a prison. The thick inside walls and window recesses have the marks of bars and heavy cell doors still on them. It now houses a museum devoted to Catalan life, costumes and folklore, a living example of which can be seen most evenings on the square before the nearby Loge de Mer. Here, during the summer at about nine o'clock in the evening, the people assemble to drink coffee and dance the great dance of Catalonia, the *Sardane*. The people of Roussillon are Catalan. French Catalan, they hasten to add, but Catalan none the less. They have strong cultural links with the Spanish Catalans across the frontier, and share with them a common language, Catalan, and of course, the *Sardane*.

Many years ago, in Spain, I spent every Sunday evening for a whole summer trying to learn the *Sardane*. It is a step-dance, where the step changes in the middle of the bar, and the beat changes in the middle of a step. It was, and still is, quite beyond me! It is a great sight to see people get up from their tables and, linking hands in a circle, young and old, trip their way through the dance to finish with a great jerk of the arms. The origins of the dance are obscure; some say the Greeks brought it to the country two thousand years ago, while

127

The Castillet at Perpignan

La Pensée by Maillol, Loge de Mer, Perpignan

others claim that it isn't very old, and started after the Napoleonic Wars. The nice thing about the *Sardane* is that it is not just danced by groups of *folklorique* performers, like an English Morris dance. Everyone does it and, on both sides of the frontier, it is the great link between the two Catalonias.

The Loge de Mer was built in the fourteenth century as a courthouse. Here all the maritime disputes could be settled. In the courtyard is another plump nude by Maillol, *La Pensée*. More intriguing is the sight of two bronze arms and a bronze hand, jutting from the outside wall. They represent the Three Estates, Lords, Clergy, People, of Roussillon, although in what precise sense I cannot imagine. Over the Loge, to emphasis the maritime connection is the fine model of a ship, serving as a weathervane. Perpignan's great artistic connection is as the birthplace of Hycinthe Rigaud, court painter to Louis XIV, who is remembered by a museum in the town. Rigaud was primarly a portrait painter, and we are indebted to him for his many paintings of the beauties at the Court of Versailles.

Not far from the Loge is the Cathedral of St. Jean, which is particularly noted for the fifteenth-century crucifix, the *Devot Christ*, in the side chapel of Notre Dame de Correchs. This crucifix, which is a work of genuine art, was once thought to be Spanish, but is now believed to be German.

Inland, some ten miles south-west of Perpignan in the Aspres hills, lies the town of Thuir, home and brewing centre of the aperitif, Byrrh. The cellars are immense, and well worth a visit.

Beyond Thuir, higher up, lies the medieval hill town of Castelnou, which is a perfect gem. No vehicles can force a way up the narrow cobbled streets and the town contains some excellent little restaurants, notably L'Oustal, which serves Catalan specialities.

The heights around Castelnou are wide and empty places with views across the plain to the mountains and the far blue sea.

East of Perpignan, the road along the Valley of the Têt leads to Prades, for many years the home of the 'cellist Pablo Casals, and on to the beautiful high plateau of the Cerdagne, the garden of the Pyrénées. On the way one can turn off to visit two abbeys, once the centre of Catalan monasticism, and now wonderfully restored. The French Pyrénées, indeed most of the remote hill country of Southern France, contains a number of abbeys of the Romanesque period, dating from the tenth or eleventh centuries. Roussillon is a storehouse of beautiful church architecture, especially of magnificent Romanesque cloisters. Romanesque, as has been mentioned elsewhere, has nothing to do with the Romans. It dates from the tenth century, being roughly contemporaneous with the Norman style found in England, taking the name from the lyrical 'Romantic' nature of the decorative carvings. The great attraction of these monasteries to the layman is in the carvings in the cloisters which, as well as being of great beauty, are often quite amusing with their allegorical scenes.

When St. Benedict established his Order and drew up the Rule of the Benedictines, which became the blueprint for medieval monastic life, he particularly urged the brethren to seek remote places for their foundations, where no secular distraction could call the brothers from their fundamental task of intercession with God. This, deep down, is the present appeal of these ancient foundations. They were built out of a belief in God and appear, as Eliot put it, as places where prayer is valid.

St. Benedict took his followers to Monte Cassino, and there at a great height, built the first of the three abbeys which have since stood there. Others quickly followed his example. The problem of the monasteries and the eventual cause of their destruction was that the monastic rule of hard work, abstinence and prayer caused them to become wealthy. A monk could not possess riches, but his Order could. The monasteries discovered that virtue was profitable. Who, nowadays, would believe that!?

St. Michel de Cuxa was consecrated in 974 A.D. and was added to progressively over the following centuries until, in the Revolution, it was burnt to the ground. The monks dispersed and it fell into ruin, and by the first years of this century was just a ruined shell. Half the cloister, which is rich in Romanesque carvings, was purchased by an American and shipped off to the Metropolitan Museum of Art, which seemed at that time to be making a cloister collection, for it also acquired half the cloister at St. Guilhem-le-Désert. However, there are moves afoot to return the cloisters of St. Guilhem and St. Michel to France and restore them to their former sites.

In the 1920s, the Cistercian Order gained possession of the Abbey and Church, and it has since been beautifully restored. The Abbey has now passed back into the care of the Benedictines, who have a pottery there.

Cloister, St Michel-de-Cuxa

Further up the valley, above Villefranche-de-Conflent, lies the second abbey, St. Martin du Canigou.

* * *

Mount Canigou is the great mountain of the Roussillon, and at eight thousand five hundred feet, is the tallest peak in the Eastern Pyrénées. Many Catalan songs recall the beauty of Mt. Canigou and in the shadow of this great peak lies the Abbey of St. Martin, a glorious example of the Romanesque. To reach it is something of a safari, as it is very remote and, after driving as far as possible, one is still left with a two mile uphill climb to tackle; no joke when laden with cameras and assorted equipment. St. Martin was established by a Count of the Cerdagne in the eleventh century and grew in wealth and beauty until, inevitably, it was abandoned during the Revolution and fell into ruin. In 1902 the Bishop of Perpignan started the work of reconstruction, and today one can see St. Martin again, in full glory. Quite apart from the church, the climb is worth it, if only to enjoy the view of the splendid surrounding peaks.

Not far from St. Martin lies the Romanesque Church of St. Etienne, at Sahorre. This is a quaint little church, again Romanesque and well worth the trip if your appetite for architecture is not yet sated.

Returning from St. Martin, the road runs through the neat little spa of Vernet-les-Bains, one of a number of spas in this part of the Pyrénées. Vernet has equipped itself for the visitor with some excellent hotels, and a large outdoor swimming pool. It is a centre for climbing and walking holidays, and for tours by jeep or landrover into Canigou, or the other peaks of the region. The old village of Vernet is well worth a visit, just to see the narrow, shady streets, and the house windows lined with flower pots.

Back to Villefranche, where time should be spared to tour this fine medieval town, fortified anew by Vauban, and a well-kept example of a French military post of the late seventeenth century. The town is earlier than the walls, and possesses *bastide* features, straight narrow streets, and narrow connecting alleys. The village, for it is hardly a town, is exceptionally clean, with clear water running continually down the gutters, as it would have done in medieval times. The town

St Michel-de-Cuxa

The walls of Villefranche de Conflent

planners of the Middle Ages always made some rudimentary efforts to keep the place clean and, since running water was their only source of power, wherever possible they would divert it down the streets, where it provided everything from drinking water to lavatories for the population. In Villefranche the sound of running water is everywhere.

Vauban is another one of those people to whom historians and writers constantly refer, without explaining who he was or what he did. Sebastian Le Prestre, Sieur de Vauban, was born in Burgundy in 1633, and entered the French Army as a sapper. Vauban was a castle-builder, a master of fortification. We noticed at Salses, that some of the ideas which he originated are in use today in the form of tank armour. Vauban adapted the medieval fortress to the age of artillery and, working at a time when Louis XIV was continually at war with his neighbours, his unique talents were in great demand. The present frontiers of France are marked out with Vauban fortresses, and it is said, whatever he built, held; whatever he besieged, fell. This is historically true, for he was also master of siege-craft. He had only to reverse his skills, concentrate not on how to make a place strong, but to search for where it was weak, and at that point his assault would be made. Curiously enough, Vauban hated war and was continually petitioning the King for permission to leave his service and become a farmer. He died in 1707.

Villefranche is a masterpiece of his military style, and still in excellent condition is the perfect place to see his work at its best.

The outer fortifications are particularly fine, well preserved, and even possess some of the original equipment. Although the drawbridge is gone, the chains and windlass remain, and the massive oak doors are still in position. Much of Villefranche is built of marble, which is quarried locally, and in the main square is a large platform of pink marble where, on Sunday evenings, the people dance the *Sardane*.

* * *

From Villefranche the road winds up, ever higher through the gorges, flanked across the abyss by the railway that links the Cerdagne with the coastal plain. This railway, running up to six thou-

135

A street in Villefranche

The bridge at Pont Séjourne

sand feet is an engineering marvel, the track having been hacked into the side of the cliffs, and the gorge spanned at intervals by beautiful and delicate viaducts, such as the Pont Séjourne, below Fontpédrouse.

Just after Fontpédrouse, a waterfall cascades for hundreds of feet down the rocks to the left, and this is the last diversion one can permit oneself, for the road is narrow, winding, and verged with a sheer drop to the valley floor far below. The French with unnatural understatement advise that it is '*Très Dangereux*', and it certainly makes you glad that you have had the brakes checked! There are parking places from time to time, and from them the views over the surrounding peaks are tremendous, but it is something of a relief to crawl over the top and arrive at Mont-Louis, the gateway to the Cerdagne.

Vauban's fortifications at Mont-Louis, which is named after Louis XIV, are much overgrown, and a poor sight after Villefranche. The town itself is a grubby little place, and at nearly five thousand

The risky road to the Cerdagne

feet, the evening air, even in summer, is too chill to permit the evening *pastis* to be taken outdoors. When the Spanish armies over-ran the Cerdagne after the French Revolution in 1793, they were repulsed outside Mont Louis by General Dagobet, and the French maintain a garrison in Mont Louis to the present day.

The Cerdagne, once the bed of a lake, was heaved up to a height of around four thousand feet by some volcanic action millions of years ago. Now it is a high, windy plateau, a sort of Shangri-La, with a climate and agriculture quite different from the plains below. Indeed, this last is the first noticeable difference. After days of endless vineyards, here it is arable farming, fruit, wheat and pasture land with herds of milky-grey Cerdagne cattle grazing in the lush grass. The houses, too, are different, more alpine, and roofed, not with the red tiles of the South, but with blue-grey slate. The Cerdagne is quite beautiful, and somehow — it's the only word for it — unexpected.

Historically, the Cerdagne has always been half French, half Spanish, wholly Catalan. The Counts of Barcelona ruled here until they themselves were extinguished, when it fell to the Kingdom of Aragon.

The French King, Louis XI, seized Roussillon in 1463, but his successor, Charles VIII, gave it back to the Catholic sovereigns Ferdinand and Isabella, in the hope of keeping them at least neutral while he went off to invade Italy. Charles had to retreat from Italy after a league of Northern Italian States was formed against him, but the Cerdagne, and all Roussillon, stayed Spanish, until the Treaty of the Pyrénées in 1659 when it passed to France. The Cerdagne does, however, still contain one anomaly from these distant days, for it contains the little Spanish town of Llivia, a Spanish enclave, several miles inside France. When the Treaty was signed, France obtained Roussillon, and thirty-three villages in the Cerdagne, but Llivia had a charter, and when the time came for it to be handed over, it was considered as a town, not a village, and therefore outside the terms of the Treaty. An example of political nit-picking that even our present times could hardly better!

One can make a circular tour of the Cerdagne, starting from Mont Louis and leading up to Bourg-Madame. The first stop is at Font Romeu, now, like much of the Pyrénées over four thousand feet, being rapidly developed into a winter sports centre. A nice touch here in the summer is the lupins. These were planted along the verges, and thrive so well, that they have become almost a weed.

The solar oven at Font-Romeu, Cerdagne

Font Romeu is a health resort, very popular for chest complaints and with children. The roads are full of great crocodiles of children toddling off on some expedition or other, and very happy they all look.

Below Font Romeu, and facing south-west, is a modern curiosity, a solar oven. This is a great saucer of reflecting mirrors, designed to concentrate the sun's rays, for the experimental solar laboratory there. It is nearly sixty yards across, a most strange sight, and must be one of the few modern scientific experiments which produces absolutely no pollution.

Having taken all this in one can proceed on to Bourg-Madame, on the frontier with Spain, and from here, back past Hix, which has a fine Romanesque church, across the Cerdagne again to Mont Louis, to complete a brief circular tour of this unique region.

It would be a pleasure to stay, but the road back lies beneath you, and a dizzy but exhilarating drive will drop you down to the coastal plain of Roussillon, or if hazardous driving thrills you, and the mountains call, then one can, from Mont Louis, head north, through the Capcir, past Formiguères, where in the fourteenth century, the Kings of Majorca came to hunt, and so on over the mountains with only eagles for company, down to the Valley of the Aude, and eventually to Quillan.

10

Rousillon, The Vallespir, and the Côtes Vermeille

From Villefranche one can head back through Prades and take the mountain road that leads over the hills to the Valley of the Têt's sister river, the Tech. This is another mountain road, even narrower than the one up to the Cerdagne and leads over the Aspres range through some wild and beautiful country, to the Priory at Serrabone. This was built in the eleventh century for the Augustine Canons by the Count of Cerdagne, and is a fine example of an early Romanesque building, set on a remote hill, giving wonderful views over the countryside. Further on, at the top of the divide, stands another church, the lonely pilgrimage Chapel of The Trinity.

This little church stands on a ridge overlooking the surrounding hills, and is, apparently, still visited by pilgrims. When I got there in the early morning it was quite deserted and yet someone must have been there, to open the beautiful iron-studded door, and light the candles within. Candles burn in racks ranged all round the sides of the church, and the floor is deep with grease below the candles, and black with smoke above.

Eventually the roads leads down, over the mountains to the town of Amélie-les-Bains, a spa in the Valley of the Tech, and gateway to the region called the Haut Vallespir. The Vallespir lies between the Canigou Massif and the Albères range, which runs along the frontier down to the sea at Port-Vendres.

Amélie looks new in this countryside of old towns, for this present town is the result of the rebuilding that took place after the cataclasmic floods of October 1940.

In summer, Languedoc-Roussillon is such a sunny, smiling place that even the occasional storm fails to shake a growing conviction that it must enjoy a mild and friendly climate all year round. The whole region carries notices beside the roads advising the traveller that in heavy rain the road will be flooded, but this seems a minor hazard compared with the Tech floods of thirty years ago, which the Michelin Guide describes as a catastrophe.

The door of the Chapel of the Trinity in the Asprès Hills

The iron door of the Trinity Chapel (detail)

In three days of October 1940, thirty inches of rain fell, and the floodwaters rose over thirty feet, in a wall of water that swept down the valley and bore all before it. All the roads were torn out, communication to the upper valley disappeared, and most of Amélie-les-Bains was submerged in the torrent.

The heavy rains naturally provoked landslides which carried away the forests on the slopes of the Tech Gorge, and anything else in their way, before they reached the valley floor, where they made dams in the flood. After a while the waters carried away the dams, and sent another tidal wave rushing down the valley. After three days the rain stopped and the floods gradually subsided. When the roads and railways were rebuilt their routes were fixed much higher up on the face of the cliffs, from where, especially at Boullanouse, the remains of the old road, carried away by a landslide, can be seen on the river bed far below. Many of the towns along the Valley today are spas, which with curative waters and pure clear air, are centres for the treatment of rheumatism, asthma, and chest complaints.

Just above Amélie lies Arles-sur-Tech, where they make excellent cakes and sweets, and one of the restaurants, *Le Relais de la Diligence,* a former coaching inn, is decorated in typical Catalan style and serves excellent regional and Spanish dishes. The town also possesses a fine Romanesque church and was the religious centre for the Haut-Vallespir, which can be covered from this spot, on a circular tour as far up the valley as Prats de Mollo.

Outside Arles, at the Gorges de la Fou, are more of the multi-coloured cliffs that recall the Tarn. The Fou gorges have to be covered on foot, along a narrow path above the river, which is a tributary of the Tech.

The road to Prats is an interesting and exciting route, which climbs steadily above the river with the Canigou range on the right, until you run at last into the outskirts of Prats-de-Mollo.

This town was fortified from the earliest times and, as a frontier town, received further attention from Vauban. The gateways are too narrow for cars, or lead to streets where a car cannot go, so it is necessary to leave it and walk around. The town is a spa, and was once the retreat of the Kings of Aragon, who built a house there, the *Maison des Rois d'Aragon*, which can be visited. The town is divided into an upper and lower town, separated by a river and linked by a very old packhorse bridge, le Pont Guilhem. Prats is a town where time stopped in the seventeenth century. The pace within the walls has to be slow, as the narrow streets wind and climb around to the circuit of the walls. Beyond lies Spain, and we must turn back again, down the valley a little way, as far as the village of Le Tech, where we fork left, up into the Canigou range to visit the town of Corsavy. From here the energetic can climb Canigou itself, but the route down to Amélie seemed risky enough to me and the evening *pastis* was calling.

*   *   *

Heading towards the coast from Amélie, the road passes through Céret, beside the high single arched medieval bridge, known as the Pont du Daible, built between 1321 and 1341. The devil seems to have had a hand in most of the bridge-building in Languedoc-Roussillon, judging from the number of bridges named after him. From the bridge one can look back to Canigou, or to the south-east, to the spur of hills called the Albères, which marks the frontier with Spain.

About the turn of the century, Céret was a mecca for such artists as

145

Picasso, Matisse and Braque, and in 1910 was known in artistic circles as the Home of Cubism. The town, which is very small, with only five thousand inhabitants, recalls those days with a Museum of Modern Art where many of these painters' works are on display, notably a fine collection of Picasso ceramics.

In the Place de la Liberty is a war memorial by the Catalan sculptor Aristide Maillol. Few towns in Roussillon are without one of his works and the traveller will soon get to recognise his opulent nudes, which can be readily identified from other nudes by having rather large legs. Maillol, who died in 1944, usually used his wife as a model, and as long as his work lasts, she, too, will never be forgotten.

From Céret the road leads down along the valley with the Albères range on the right, across the route of the new motorway, to St. Martin de Fenollar, which lies at the foot of the pass which leads into Spain at Le Perthus. Down this pass came Hannibal, on his way to invade Italy, and before that, in the Heroic Age, Hercules passed over into Spain by Le Perthus, seeking the Golden Apples of the Hesperides, believed nowadays to have been Seville oranges, which is a neat explanation, but has nothing like the same romantic appeal. I can't believe that anyone would go to all that trouble for an *orange*. A Golden Apple—that's something else again!

Through Bains du Boulou, and across country brings one through Elne and to the Côte Vermeille, the name given to the strip of coast, sandy and rocky, roughly between Argelès and Cerbère. In the summer months this coast is packed with holiday-makers, but even a little way inland it is comparatively easy to find accommodation.

The question of where to stay in Languedoc-Roussillon has not yet been covered, and in such a large area, is a question not easily answered, but a good start is to obtain the hotel guide to the *Logis de France*. For anywhere in France, except Paris, which they do not include, the *Guide des Logis de France* is invaluable.

This guide lists at present over three thousand five hundred very comfortable, moderately priced family hotels, in country districts, and the Logis always give good value. If there is no *Logis* in the area, reference can be made to the Michelin Red Guide. However, not all hotels are in either *Logis* or Michelin, and if the traveller shops around a little he can usually obtain accommodation somewhere and at a reasonable price. French hotels generally are cheaper than those in England, and offer better value for money, for usually every bedroom is equipped with a bath or shower, and the rates shown are

Constantines emblem in the cloister at Elne

firm. There are no nasty extras to inflate the bill next morning. While one cannot fault the advice to book in advance, this wouldn't suit my style of travelling, which is to wander, never knowing from day to day, quite where I will end up, and so I never book.

I have been travelling in or through France for many years now, and have always found somewhere to stay. If a place seems really crowded, as it can be on the coast in summer, then my advice is to head inland. Almost every French village has some sort of hotel, and before long you will find something. It is, however, good advice not to wait until too late in the evening.

Apart from hotels, many people tour with a caravan. This is an excellent way of seeing the country, and as Languedoc-Roussillon has over five hundred officially listed camp sites, with all the best features of French camp sites, plus perhaps twice as many private sites, here again, while the official advice to book, especially during July and August, cannot be faulted, I have visited many sites and usually found that some space was still available. Besides, it's a big country, and if one place is too crowded, then there will always be room somewhere else.

This coast, as elsewhere along the littoral, is being developed for the yachtsman, notably with excellent marinas at Canet-Plage, St. Cyprian, and Argeles. In Canet, which is the largest centre of the three, the Hotel Escale is a particularly fine, small hotel, without a restaurant, but with excellent accommodation.

*   *   *

Another good centre for touring the Côte Vermeille is the little village of St. Cyprian. The Hotel Belvedere there is strategically situated on a hill by the water tower, from which great views are offered towards the coast or the Pyrénées. Nearby lies the town of Elne, once the capital of Roussillon, and now a quiet pleasant town with at least one good restaurant, the Carrefour, offering regional dishes.

In early Roman times, the town was called *Illiberis* and, at the end of the era, was renamed *Castrum Helenae,* in honour of Helen, mother of the Emperor Constantine, who found the True Cross in Jerusalem. The present name of Elne is derived from this.

The town remained the centre of the local bishopric until 1602, when the bishop moved to Perpignan, but the great Cathedral

Church, which dates from the eleventh century, still stands, and possesses the most complete and beautifully decorated Romanesque cloister in this part of France, which can be viewed, incidentally, without a guide, or a leg-testing climb up a mountain.

The carvings are very clear, showing saints and soldiers, St. Peter preaching or in prison, and, a nice touch, here and there one sees the hand of God popping out of a cloud to give a quick blessing to the mortals below. One wall bears Constantine's symbol, the Labarum, which appeared to him in a dream and, painted on his banners and the shields of his soldiers, always gave him victory.

The church is earlier than the cloister, but has been much restored. On one wall of the nave hangs an enormous processional cross embellished with the articles of the Passion and Crucifixion. The scourge, the nails, the shroud, the lance and vinegar sponge, are all hanging up, a touch of Spain, and a visual reminder to the faithful which fits in well with the usual gloomy Gothic setting.

*　　*　　*

The gem of the Côte Vermeille is the beautiful port of Collioure. Collioure developed as a trading port in Greek times, and enjoyed great

The carvings in the cloisters, Elne

The descent from the Cross, cloister, Elne

prosperity during the Middle Ages. A Spanish town, it passed to France in 1642, and the mighty Templar castle by the harbour, built against the Saracen pirates was promptly rebuilt as a frontier bastion by Vauban. It now contains a training centre for the French Commandos.

The most noticeable sight in Collioure, and the focus of every eye, is the old Phare, or lighthouse, built by the side of the church. The church dates from the seventeenth century, but the Phare, now a clock-tower, although very appropriately the clock has stopped, predates the church by some three hundred years.

The Château and the Phare divide up the stony beaches of the town, which begin with the Plage St. Vincent, by the mole. Then follows the Plage du Vieux Port, and, after the castle, the Plage de la Balette. Behind the Vieux Port are rows of restaurants, little bars and shops, braced against the old walls, through which arched gateways admit you to the alleyways and streets of the old town.

The whole area abounds with colour; pink roofs, sea blue and clear to the bottom, and criss-crossed with the coloured sails of pleasure craft and the wakes of speed boats.

It has to be faced that Collioure has brought the crowds down on itself, and is strangling in their grip. The undoubted prosperity that the summer brings to the town makes it an infernally noisy and congested place at the same time. It is better to visit the place in the autumn or late spring, when, more peacefully, you can imagine what it was like when the painters discovered it in the 1900's.

Collioure was first noticed by the 'Fauves', that group of painters which included Rouault, Derain, Matisse and Vlaminck. Their bold colours and sweeping strokes so enraged one Paris critic after the Exhibition of 1905, that he called them the 'Wild Beasts', or 'Fauves', a name the group was happy to answer to. Matisse lived in the resort for many years, and was soon joined by Picasso and Dufy, many of whose pictures, with little boats on a bright sea, breathe the air of Collioure. Many of the painters, for accommodation or the price of a meal, gave a painting to the principal hotel, the Hostellerie des Templars, where they hang on the walls of the dining room today, a fine collection of early Modern Art. There are artists, of varying merit, in the town today, and they can be seen at work in the little streets and coves around the town or harbour. From the harbour the fishing boats go out each night, many of the smaller ones fishing *à la lamparo*, with a large pressure-lantern hung over the side, to entice

Collioure

Maillol memorial to the war-dead, Banyuls

curious fish into their nets. On a soft night, from the Albères, the hills behind Collioure, the lights can be seen sparkling far out on the sea.

*   *   *

From Collioure to the frontier is a short run, over the edge of the Albères range, first to Port-Vendres, now a port for North Africa and the Balearics. A ferry runs from Port Vendres to Alcudia in Majorca, three times a week in the summer. Port-Vendres has a huge terminal building, large enough to absorb the passenger trade of a Transatlantic port, and several good sea-food restaurants. From here it is only a few miles to Banyuls, home of the local wine, a heavy port-like drink, often drunk as an aperitif. Banyuls is a great place for sailing, and has an impressive war memorial by Maillol, and a Marine laboratory and aquarium named after François Arago, a native of Perpignan, and a noted astronomer. He has a statue in Per-

153

Rigging a boat at Banyuls

pignan, and quite why Banyuls should name an aquarium after him is a trifle obscure, but there it is, and one can visit it. The inside is dark, damp and decidedly fishy, but full of interesting exhibits.

In the aquarium, deep in the damp gloom, live a variety of undersea creatures, many too obscure for the layman to identify. Great crabs nip off sideways, and a giant congar eel glares evilly up at you.

We can't finish a visit to Languedoc-Roussillon in a dark void like this!

Outside again then, back past the dinghies, setting sail on the hard, and out on the road to Cèrbere and the frontier.

The traffic is intense, and swiftly handled, so that it is difficult to avoid being swept across the border in this mechanical flood.

I pulled off the road, and watched the traffic beat past. So many German cars were flooding over the frontier that it looked like an invasion. Down below lay the Mediterranean, and it took only a few moments to run across the rocks, roll up the trousers, and wash off the dust of travel in the warm blue sea.

Finis

Bibliography

Southern France by Maurice Rosenbaum, published by Thornton Cox, 1975.

Michelin Red Guide to France — current year's edition.

Guide des Auberges et Logis de France — current year's edition.

Guide de Relais Routiers — current year's edition.

Michelin Green Guides (French version).
Causses, Bas-Languedoc, Cévennes,
Provence, Pyrenees, Auvergne.

West of the Rhône by Freda White, published by Faber, 1964.

History, People and Places in The Dordogne by Neil Lands, published by Spurbooks, 1975.

Travels with a Donkey in the Cévennes by R. Louis Stevenson, 1898.

Languedoc by George Savage, published by Barrie & Jenkins, 1975.

A Concise History of France, published by Cassell.

A History of the Knights Templar by G.A. Campbell, published by Duckworth, 1937.

Companion Guide to Southern France by Archibald Lyall, published by Collins, 1963.

A Holiday History of France by Ronald Hamilton, published by Chatto & Windus, 1971.

Roussillon by Yves Hoffman.

Good maps are essential and the Tourist maps of the Institute Geographic National Nos. 11 and 14 are recommended and can be obtained from Stanfords Ltd., Long Acre, London WC1.

Index

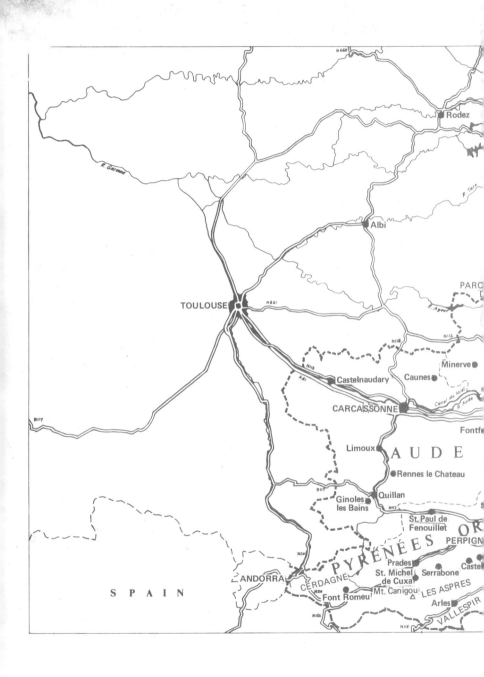